Adoption
The Inside Story

For all adopted children and their parents

From left to right: Eric, Simon, Jo, Nicola and Dan.

Adoption
The inside story

Edited by
Judy Austin
for
Parent to Parent
Information on Adoption Services

Barn Owl Books

© Parent to Parent Information on Adoption Services
1985

First published 1985 by
Barn Owl Books
Westowe Farmhouse
Lydeard St Lawrence
Taunton
Somerset

Reprinted with corrections 1987

British Library Cataloguing in Publication Data

Adoption: the inside story.
  1. Adoption
  I. Austin, Judy II. Parent to Parent
Information on Adoption Services
  364.7'34'0922   HV875

  ISBN 0-9509057-3-9

Typeset in 10 on 11 point Century and
9 on 10 Helios
Typeset by Colset Private Ltd, Singapore
Printed and bound by Richard Clay
(The Chaucer Press) Ltd,
Bungay, Suffolk

Contents

	Acknowledgements	vi
	Foreword by David Bellamy	vii
	Introduction by John Fitzgerald	ix
	Editor's preface	xii
Chapter 1	Assessment and preparation	1
Chapter 2	Living with handicap	11
Chapter 3	Adopting babies	21
Chapter 4	The terrible twos: adopting toddlers	28
Chapter 5	The turbulent teens: adopting teenagers	34
Chapter 6	Changing places: introducing another child into an existing family	45
Chapter 7	A ready-made family	52
Chapter 8	Bonding: letting the love grow	61
Chapter 9	Telling: sharing the past	71
Chapter 10	Keeping in touch: adoption with contact	81
Chapter 11	Tracing	89
Chapter 12	Transracial adoption	98
Chapter 13	Institutionalized children	111
Chapter 14	Adopted children at school	119
Chapter 15	Single parents	129
Chapter 16	Contested cases	138
Chapter 17	Disruption	146
Chapter 18	Tales of the unexpected	156
Chapter 19	The last word: the comments of adoptees	164
	Further reading	175
	Useful addresses	176
	Index	177

Acknowledgements

I am very grateful to the following people who have helped in the preparation of this book: Pauline Jones for typing the manuscript, and Bernard Cooknell for photocopying it; Sheilagh Crawford for her assistance in the initial stages; Hilary Cain for her professional advice as a social worker; and Philly Morrall for her incredible patience and support.

Finally, on behalf of PPIAS, I should like to thank the families whose stories and photographs have created this book, not forgetting all the other adoptive families whose contributions to the PPIAS Newsletter over the years have provided such invaluable inspiration and encouragement to others.

Judy Austin

Foreword

David Bellamy

When asked to write a foreword to a book about adoption and fostering, my first private reaction was to say, 'Oh no.' Human relationships of this type are so personal, and hence so complex and diverse, that no book is going to be able to do them justice. So many bland statements will be made, so many aspects will be omitted, that it will hinder, not help, prospective parents.

How wrong could I be? Here is a work of real understanding, written with a deep appreciation and concern for humanity as it can only come to fruition through the real sense of family.

Why should I write the foreword? What are my credentials? In the knowledge that the world is already overpopulated, and not wanting to compound the problem with too many Bellamys, we decided to have two children of our own and adopt two. We ended up with a multinational family of five, four adopted through the Church of England Children's Society, known in our home as 'the Building Society'.

Being somewhat in the public eye, I am also invited to visit many children's homes, hostels, and adoption centres of all types. I don't like doing it because they always make me feel broody. I always want to take all the children home. It also makes me feel inadequate when I meet people who have dedicated their lives to such institutions, and to fostering babies and children with all types of problem and handicap.

I also know what it is like to be in a 'no children situation', and what it is like to lose one when you have just got it, and so understand the anguish of the ever-growing number of childless couples, and the trials and disappointments of the waiting list and adoption procedure. I also know and understand the problems of acceptance of and adjustment to a new member of the family.

The biology of the human species means that life in an institution, however well run, is no substitute for a real home with real family bonds. However, the creation of that real home and those real bonds doesn't just happen, and much hard work is needed on all sides. There is disappointment more often than not in any human relationship. The only real problem is when disappointment in oneself turns into recrimination, rather than into a resolve to accept that to err is human, and that to admit and forgive is the basis of the family unit, the most precious thing that we can ever achieve.

My apologies — I am trying to do what I said was impossible: trying to summarize the joys and fears of letting another human being become part of you.

Every month I get several letters asking about adoption: why have we been so lucky? what were the real problems? how do the children get on? what about the grandparents, neighbours, colleagues at work? To date I have always sweated long over my answers. I need worry no more. This book is a classic in human understanding, a pied piper of a text that will lead you on to make the right decisions for you and your future family.

In 'The Ascent of Man' Jacob Bronowski said, 'Sometimes we must touch humanity.' This book touches it again and again. I hope every library will get a number of copies, for every family will benefit from its practical compassion.

Bedburn, 1985

Introduction

John Fitzgerald

In preparation for writing this introduction I had the opportunity to read all the chapters in this book, and in many ways the experience was rather like a trip down memory lane. I found my mind going back to all of the children and families I had known, and to how each story was in its own way unique.

My first experience of the adoption world was as an administrator in 1966; and – although I did not realize it at the time – my career was to span 19 years (to date), during which the adoption scene was to undergo extraordinary change. The mid-1960s were the 'boom' years for healthy white baby adoptions, and special needs placements were still only the figment of a few enlightened imaginations.

Today we can trace the changes through the years:

- very few healthy white babies needing adoptive parents now, compared with the 1960s; an apparently greater number of infertile people who will not be able to parent a baby;
- the development of an awareness within adoption agencies that the child with special needs, such as those with severe mental or physical handicaps, emotionally damaged older children, groups of brothers and sisters, can benefit from adoptive family life;
- a shift by adoption agencies away from 'vetting' would-be adoptive parents to a more open 'educative' approach;
- the development of new recruitment techniques, such as the use of television, adoption parties, use of photographs in publicity, to find new families for children with special needs;
- the development of local authority adoption services to meet the changing needs; the change in services amongst voluntary agencies; and the establishment of new specialist organizations such as Parents for Children;
- the major changes in legislation contained within the Children's Act 1975 which provided for adoptees to obtain their birth certificate at 18 years of age; in some areas subsidized adoptions through 'approved

Adoption: the inside story

adoption allowances'; 'freeing' which is intended to streamline the legal/administrative process of adoption; (sadly, some sections are still awaiting implementation);
- the move to ensure that wherever possible black children are placed within their own communities.

These changes may now be part of the adoption scene, but each one has been accompanied by more than a little controversy and some considerable pain. Those involved, for example, in the use of television to feature a child needing an adoptive family in 1974, when 'World in Action' produced a documentary on the subject, will testify to the at times vitriolic coverage by the rest of the media, and the ambivalence or the downright hostility from within the social work profession. And currently, the heat generated around transracial adoption has a familiar ring to it.

However, involved in and influencing each of these changes in the adoption scene has been an active and enthusiastic adoptive parents' organization, Parent to Parent Information on Adoption Services. As well as, and at times because of, its role in providing support and information services to adoptive parents, it has continually found itself helping to push back the boundaries of what is possible for children and families alike. It is interesting to speculate on whether it would now be possible for adopted people in England and Wales (Scotland already had this facility) to obtain their birth certificates had not PPIAS supported the change in legislation during the passage of the bill that ultimately was to become the Children's Act 1975. I wonder!

Over the years PPIAS has published a marvellous Newsletter with, amongst other things, details of children waiting for new families. Indeed, this Newsletter was the first regular 'photolisting' of waiting children in this country. However, it is really the written experiences of adoptive parents which this book is about. Each Newsletter contained short pieces written by adoptive parents describing their experiences, sometimes the joy of adoption, others the pain or

Introduction

frustration. Sometimes there were bouquets for the professionals (from across a range of disciplines), on other occasions severe and at times sadly justified criticisms.

This book contains a selection of those short articles covering the current range of adoption services, plus some comments from a few children. Re-reading the familiar stories reminded me of the joy and the pain of those who 'live' adoption; they capture the love, courage, humour and sometimes sadness of building a new family. They made me marvel again at how much the professionals like me owe to the amazing families who in many cases coped with and loved the children many would have given up on long ago.

PPIAS initiatives have not always been welcomed by the professionals responsible for delivering adoption services; but I hope this book will demonstrate the strength of PPIAS, and why professional services alone can never be enough.

Editor's preface

PPIAS was formed in 1971 by a group of adoptive parents, primarily to support and advise families hoping to adopt children then considered 'hard to place'. In order to give these families the benefit of the first-hand experiences of seasoned adopters, an information exchange was set up; and there are now about 90 local groups operating in Great Britain. Since 1972 a Newsletter has been circulated to members three times a year. Each edition contains photographs and details of children needing permanent new families, information on general developments in fostering and adoption, and the real-life stories of adoptive families.

The aim of this book has been to bring together a selection of those stories and, in doing so, to give readers an overall view of the adoption world as seen through the eyes of adopters. It is not a step by step account of *how* to adopt but it will, I hope, provide a real taste of how it feels to build a family by adoption.

The book has been arranged so that each chapter deals with a different aspect of adoption, for easy reference. Some accounts, however, cover more than one aspect, and anyone dipping into the book selectively for specific topics would be advised to consult the index as well as the chapter titles.

Finally, I have been asked by some of the families to make the point that their lives have changed since they wrote these pieces. Indeed, it would be unusual if they had not. In some cases the children have grown up and left home; in others new children have been added. Sometimes, sadly, problems have arisen or, in happier cases, been resolved. Nevertheless, all of the stories included in this book describe experiences and feelings which were absolutely genuine at the time.

Judy Austin

CHAPTER 1

Assessment and preparation

When a couple decide to apply to a local authority or independent adoption agency to be assessed as prospective adoptive parents, they have taken the first step in what can be either an educative and illuminating experience or just a frustrating and nerve-racking one. Once called 'vetting' and now more appropriately named 'assessment', the process is inevitably an emotionally tiring one, since so much — the child or children for whom the couple long — depends on the outcome.

In the articles in this chapter, several PPIAS families have outlined what the procedure was like for them. Put together, their accounts give some idea of how much this crucial stage in adoption can vary. Much seems to depend on what the social worker is like, and how much time she or he has to offer the clients! But whatever sort of treatment a couple receive — and even if they are relaxed and their social worker sympathetic, so that they don't feel as if they are being 'tested' — the day the adoption panel meets to discuss their application might feel a little like the day on which the examination results are posted. Some couples who, after discussion with their social worker, feel that adoption is not for them drop out before this stage. All those who continue with their assessment should be given some idea by their social worker of the likely outcome when the panel meets. Even so, a couple whose application is not accepted must inevitably be disappointed. It is a time when they desperately need further counselling and practical, constructive advice. Couples who are 'approved' will, understandably, be euphoric for a while and, if they have been prepared for a specific child, introductions may begin. If, however, *their* child has yet to materialize, they could face another frustrating stage in the adoption process — their names go on to the agency's list — and the wait begins. This could be a few months, if they are lucky, or a year or more. It can be a frustrating time, but worth it in the end!

Adoption: the inside story

● Our experiences of assessment, nine, eight and five years ago, were scanty, to say the least, by today's standards. We were interviewed by a neighbouring local authority, and the social worker said that she liked to do three interviews at weekly intervals (two together and one each separately). All the interviews were held in an ante-room, out of which led the offices of five other social workers – who were constantly popping in and out, apologizing profusely as they did so!

The social worker was a pleasant and sensitive woman in her fifties whom we liked, but who, I guessed (and she later confirmed), had recently had a nervous breakdown: she was as thin as a rake and a chain-smoker; she sat on the very edge of her chair and talked incessantly; she was quite the least relaxing person I had ever met! We spent our time sitting back and willing her to relax – perhaps we succeeded a little, because she did say at the end, 'You're very easy to talk to, you two.' As the social worker was such a compulsive talker, she had hardly any time to ask us any questions; at least, she did ask a few, but she didn't have time to wait for the answers: she asked us, 'How would you feel about the child of a prostitute?' and then was off on another story about a prostitute's child that she had recently placed.

Before going for our interviews, we had spent months thinking and talking about adopting a child of a different race, visiting PPIAS mixed-race families, reading all the literature we could obtain etc., so when she asked us, 'What about colour?' we said, 'Any colour', and were prepared for quite a grilling on the subject: but no – she wrote it down, and was then off on another anecdote. She never asked us if we had any black friends or neighbours, any knowledge of African or Caribbean cultures, how our friends and family would react, or indeed how we ourselves would feel about a child with a different skin colour. I did both ring her and write subsequently, telling her the answers to some of the questions we thought she ought to have asked! In our solo interviews we were asked in minute detail about the chronology of our early lives, exam results, jobs done etc., but never were we asked anything about our marriage, relationships with our families, or whether there were any differences between us in our ideas about adoption or possibly in our reactions to the child we might have.

Four months after this we were 'on the list', and nine months later we were offered a six-week-old healthy white infant of educated parents.

We had two further interviews for each of two subsequent

children. We had a different (and very nice) social worker who saw us in a small private office, asked us most of the relevant questions – and waited for us to answer! We were never interviewed separately again. I think this should always be done; however many children a couple adopt, marriages change – especially as more children arrive – and there may be areas of thought and feeling that are not shared by the couple and probably will not surface in a discussion 'à trois'. We have our family – one white and two brown – but I don't know if we would ever get on the list in today's rigorous climate.

1984

- In 1977 an assessment of our family for adoption of a healthy child under four seemed like a normal, though unnerving, step towards the goal of having a second child. We did not question how the assessment was conducted because we had no idea of others' experiences and even less of our own expectations. We followed an apparently acceptable pattern of a formal interview between ourselves and a social worker in an office at the headquarters of the independent agency to which we had applied, and a series of meetings (some as a family and some as individuals) with the same social worker in our own home. We were told at the first interview of the general situation as regards babies (of which we were already aware after a fair amount of previous thought and research into the adoption field), and the kinds of children for whom agencies were seeking families. We were advised to go away and think about it, and if, after six months, we felt we had something to offer, to come back. I think that six months was, in reality, six days, as we had already done our thinking, and because our regular receipt of the PPIAS Newsletter had already helped us understand that we did have something to offer to some of the children featured. There followed some five or six visits from the social worker, who, at the outset, I had felt *must* be too young and too inexperienced in *anything* to know if we, who were after all already tried and proven as adequate natural parents, would also be adequate adoptive parents. However, he proved to be astute, caring, amusing and wise beyond my expectations! He turned out to be all those things and more – about 18 months after our first tentative letter we were presented with an eight-week-old mixed-parentage son!

However, on reflection, and having had many chances since to talk to others who have been 'vetted', we realized only too clearly how lucky we were. If the terminology used is somewhat daunting and offputting – 'vetting' should be struck off the list of adoption jargon, and 'assessment' is not much better – at least we were spared the treatment that threatens to go with such words. We do not remember being asked more than one direct question, or being confused by jargon, and certainly our social worker never wrote a note whilst he was with us – our interviews were just very wide discussions. 'Our man' had a long journey to reach us, so we generally arranged for him to come over a meal-time. This gave us all something to do, and reduced any tension there might have been. My range of cooking is limited to what you can do with a pound of mince or a chicken, so he didn't get excited by my culinary prowess. We also realized that you don't have to be a Cordon Bleu cook to parent a child! We were nervous, of course, but he was easy and friendly without being unprofessional or sloppy, and it was definitely one of the better experiences of a 'conventional vetting'. Two questions have always remained unanswered, though. Would we feel so good about exactly the same easy relaxed interviews if ultimately we hadn't 'got what we wanted'? And, at the time we were both smokers (now reformed and horribly smug); we always smoked with our social worker over cups of coffee, etc., and when offered a cigarette, he too smoked. But . . . he never had his own! Was he too poor, or did he just smoke to make us feel less bad about such a habit? Either way, we remain half-amused and half-puzzled. Thank you, Mr Jones, wherever you are now!

1984

- We have a child of our own, Michael, who is nearly three years old. We wanted to add to our family, so we thought of adopting a mentally handicapped child or baby. We went to our social services department, to no avail. The social worker was very offputting, so we both went home, thinking to give it all up. We did, for a year.

    Then we thought, 'No! Why should we give up?' So we wrote to Parents for Children, who sent us photos of children they were finding homes for at that time. We saw a little girl we liked, so we wrote off. The social worker phoned us up, and we went for an interview. The social worker made us very welcome. She told us that there were other families who wanted to know about the little girl we had come to see on the video, but she also told us that we could always go down and see if there was another child

Assessment and preparation

or baby, should *we* feel the little girl wasn't for us, or should *they* feel that she wasn't for us. No-one is turned away. The social worker said that there is always a child for someone. My husband and I would never go to the social services again for a child. We are going to stick with the voluntary agency, because they were understanding.

1984

- For a long time we had both wanted to offer a home to children with special needs, who needed a family. When we met and got married, adopting children seemed the most natural step to take, more important than having children of our own (although, as far as we know, we can have children of our own).

  In December 1980 we approached our nearest social services department, who had also just advertised for adoptive parents in *New Society*. At that time, I was 22 and my husband 29. We filled in a few questionnaires and were invited to a preliminary chat with a social worker. After that nothing happened for ages, until we were invited to a series of group meetings with other interested people. We felt rather out of place at these meetings, since it was quite clear that the SSD were looking for a particular type of couple, a mould we did not easily fit. Again, nothing happened after those meetings for a long time, apart from the SSD's collecting the necessary papers and our having a medical.

  When we finally met our social worker to begin the formal assessment process, ten months had passed by since our first inquiry. The assessment itself was an absolute waste of time from our point of view. During five or six meetings, we hardly got any further than discussing age, sex, colour, number of children we wanted. The social worker could never remember, despite taking pages and pages of notes, what we had said during the previous meetings, and she was always too much in a hurry because of other appointments to talk about some of the things we wanted to talk about. After each of those meetings we felt utterly frustrated, but at that stage we were too inexperienced to ask for another social worker. All the time we were made to feel that we were not really important, that we had nothing to offer a child, but only that the SSD had something to offer to us, a child. Therefore, we had to be good and do as we were told, or else we would be turned down.

  We had been told that the adoption panel met on alternate Thursdays, but not which Thursdays. So, once the assessment process had been completed, we waited for a phone call on each and every Thursday for three long months. Needless to say, we were turned down. We were, of course, shattered, yet not altogether surprised about the result. After all, we had not felt that the social worker had understood our decision to adopt rather than have children of our own. The social worker tried to explain some of the reasons as to why we had been turned down, some rather ludicrous, e.g. that we would be moving to another part of the country in four years' time and that would be too short a period of time in which to place a child; that I was really too young; and indirectly, that my husband's income as a clergyman was not large enough. Since all this information was known to the SSD right from the outset, we could not help but feel somewhat cheated. The whole process had taken 18 months. We were no further on, apart from being as determined as ever that we wanted to adopt and would look for another agency.

We approached Dr Barnardo's, and the difference in the approach towards the assessment process was unbelievable. We made our first inquiry in June 1982, and were accepted in December of the same year. We talked about all kinds of aspects of adoption in general, and the kinds of children needing placements in particular. The social worker brought us books to read, and organized visits to a children's home and to a foster family. There was never a rush during any of those meetings, which, incidentally, all took place at our own home, and after each one we felt we had become a little clearer about our decision and what was involved. It was also *we* who could talk about what concerned, worried *us*, rather than having the social worker arrive with a catalogue of questions that had to be got through. We were also invited to a number of group meetings, and could not believe our eyes when we saw the mixture of people present; they came in all shapes and sizes and ages, and some were even unemployed!

Once the assessment process had been completed, we were told the date of the next adoption panel, and even the approximate time our social worker would ring with the decision. This time we were successful, and since November 1983 we have been the proud parents of a five-and-a-half-year-old, mentally handicapped boy, whose photograph we first saw in the *Be My Parent* book.

We certainly have nothing but praise for the way Dr Barnardo's in general, and our social worker in particular, have helped and supported us during the assessment process, the initial placement of our son, and the support we continue to

Assessment and preparation

receive. It is this kind of help and support that has given us the confidence to accept both the frustrations and joys that an addition to our family has brought. Our first experience has also taught us not to take this support for granted.

1984

- Leroy's page in the *Be My Parent* book was not flattering, to say the least; in fact it was downright offputting. The picture showed an unhappy looking little Anglo/West Indian boy with glasses too big for his little face. The only complimentary comment his description made was that he was lovable. In fact Leroy was not the type of child we *thought* we were looking for! However, for some reason he struck a chord, and we inquired about him. Leroy was very fortunate in having a social worker who was committed to finding a family for him. She was most enthusiastic when we spoke to her and thought we sounded just right for him. (We later learned that she was pretty desperate, as nobody else had inquired about him!)

She visited us just before Christmas 1981, and confirmed her opinion that we were the 'right' family for Leroy. We were asked to think it over and let her know after Christmas whether we wished to proceed. The decision was not hard to make; we 'knew' that he was right for our family. The assessment began towards the end of January 1982. It was conducted by a colleague of Leroy's social worker.

The social worker herself felt that she could not be objective enough, as she was very fond of Leroy and very anxious to place him. We found that there was an immediate rapport between ourselves and the assessment social worker. We had about six visits in all, in which she interviewed us together and separately. We enjoyed her visits, which we found thought-provoking. If an assessment is done properly (as ours was), it makes one look at one's relationships and motives in a depth in which one does not normally think. The social worker was very frank with us and we were equally frank with her. We were able to look at our family from the outsider's point of view, which was very interesting. We asked for, and were given, a copy of the social worker's report on us. It was a fairly flattering report which made us all glow, we sounded so nice!

The great day came towards the end of April, when we were approved by the adoption panel. A blind viewing was arranged to see if we still wanted Leroy; this confirmed that he was the right child for us. There was some delay before visits could begin, as his key worker was ill, and it was felt that Leroy needed the support of his worker during the handover period. Leroy was told a couple of days before the first official visit that he had a new family. He was so excited that he immediately phoned up and said 'Hello, Mummy, when can I come and live with you?' The visits went well and he was able to have his ninth birthday party at our home. Two weeks later, Leroy moved in for good.

From the moment Leroy moved in, it was like a piece of jigsaw fitting into place; he belonged. It had been agreed that we should foster him for nine months before we adopted him. No problem was envisaged in getting Leroy freed for adoption by his authority's local council; it was expected to go through on the nod. Then the bombshell dropped! The new black chairman of the council was by no means certain that a white middle-class family would do much to make Leroy aware of his black identity. We had been aware that there was a move to end transracial adoptions, but had not considered that we might be affected. Leroy was our son, and we would fight tooth and nail to adopt him! Fortunately, Leroy's Social Services thought the same way, and the delay in getting him freed for adoption proved to be a hiccup. The rest of the adoption process went smoothly; the guardian ad litem, although very thorough (we had about five visits as comprehensive as our original assessment), was very pleasant, and we eventually went to court on 28 July 1983, the day before Leroy's tenth birthday. The judge was in chambers and in a lounge suit – much to the children's disappointment! However the box of chocolates thoughtfully provided on his desk did much to mitigate their disappointment at not seeing him dressed up! Afterwards we celebrated with the Guardian ad Litem with cokes and cakes all round at the nearest cafe. Then for the moment Leroy had been waiting for – we went to order nametapes in his new name. I think that was the highlight of his day!

1984

- We have had plenty of experience of home studies, as we have now been under the microscope four times – once by an adoption agency in this country in order to get on their list, and three times during the adoption of our baby son from Brazil! The agency study was a long-drawn-out procedure which lasted about 18 months, during which we would see our social worker, say, every six to eight weeks for about an hour. During these sessions she would ask us obvious questions like 'Would you go out and leave your baby alone in the house at night?' and 'Do you believe in spanking a child?' Anyone with an ounce of intelligence could have given the 'correct' answers on cue, and I don't believe she ever really discovered our innermost thoughts and feelings. This is shown by the fact that we were approved as suitable to adopt an older child or children, when we really wanted a baby or toddler (impossible in the UK because of age limits).

In contrast, our privately commissioned home study for our overseas adoption was over in three intensive visits, and on reading the final report we were amazed at how well the social worker had understood us. In nine well-written pages she had summarized our lives, education and work experience to date, our marriage and our attitude to one another and our hopes for a family of our own, together with what we expected from the child, each other, and our friends and relations. She had interviewed each of us alone, and then together, and it was interesting to discover how we viewed one another and our marriage – some of her questions really made us think.

Once we knew the baby was ours in Brazil, we had to apply for entry clearance (permission to bring him into the UK for adoption under UK law). In order to assess whether an adoption order would be likely to be granted, the DHSS required our local social services to do – guess what – another home study on us. Our adoption agency refused to release our details to the social services, so we had to cover all the same ground again. Luckily, they were willing to use our private home study as the basis for their report, so they only had to make two or three token visits to clear up any queries they had, plus the usual health and police checks. I must say, they really made an effort to push things through quickly, knowing that the baby was waiting for us to collect him.

Finally, once we had our baby at home, we had three or four more visits from the social services (called welfare visits) to assess how we were caring for him. They don't seem to have any alternative procedures for overseas adoptions, and the social worker didn't really know what she was supposed to be checking on. Even if we had been mistreating the baby, they would have had problems taking him away from us, as he was still a Brazilian citizen and legally adopted by us under Brazilian law!

To summarize – a home study is a useful procedure for allowing an outside person to report on a couple's suitability to adopt a child, but it is relatively easy for the average person to conceal or reveal facts and feelings as they choose. We did not find that the studies helped us to prepare for adoption, but then we had already thought carefully and made our decision to adopt long ago. It was simply a question of going through all the necessary procedures to achieve our aim.

1984

CHAPTER 2

Living with handicap

The previous chapter described what it is like being assessed and prepared as adopters. This and the following chapters will give you some idea of what can happen once your child or children have arrived! Naturally this will depend on the age and type of child you have adopted, and on the structure of your existing family.

Many of the children needing permanent new families today are handicapped in some way. For some children the handicap is an emotional one: they have behavioural problems, and find it difficult to form lasting relationships because of the unsettled lives they have led. Others may have a mental or physical disability which may be coupled with emotional problems as well. Children who are handicapped mentally or physically were once considered 'unadoptable', but many do now find new parents who have the strength, patience and love to cope with their very special needs. Independent agencies, like Parents for Children in London, as well as some local authority adoption units, are extremely experienced in preparing 'special needs' children and their prospective parents for adoption, and in supporting placements after the adoption orders have been granted.

Most couples who decide to adopt a handicapped child do so with their eyes open; but two of the families who have written about their experiences for us discovered their child's disability only after the placement had been made. Here they describe how they faced the news, where they turned for support and what sort of reactions they met from others. What draws a family to adopt a handicapped child? Our contributors answer this and outline what, for them, have been the challenges and rewards of 'living with handicap'.

Adoption: the inside story

- Nicholas came to us first as a long-term foster child. He is severely brain-damaged, blind, partially deaf, mildly spastic and probably mentally handicapped. Before he had been with us for six months, he had so entwined himself round all our hearts (we have four normally born teenagers of normal intelligence and physical attributes) that we couldn't bear the thought of his ever being taken from us, possibly to be put into residential hospital care against our wishes. We discussed all the implications with the older children, and unanimously agreed to apply to adopt Nicholas (knowing that his mother didn't want him), although he was never offered for adoption.

  His progress has been quite remarkable. His hearing has increased, his sense of humour has developed, his tactile development is such that if a very small vibration is made in front of him he 'looks' for what made it with his hands. He is trying to feed himself (what a mess!) and we hope that with persistent physiotheraphy and speech therapy he will both walk and talk. We have been given unlimited help and support from social workers and doctors.

  He came to us at six months, as a little wailing bundle, but the adjustment was no more than it would have been in having a normal new baby at our time of life. Many friends thought we were crazy – a few, who are crazy themselves, think we are saints! Neither is correct. We have a worthwhile job, a most rewarding relationship, and such a lot of love throughout the family. It would be dishonest to say that our relationship with Nicholas is all pleasure – there is a lot of pain involved in it as well – but what relationship between parent and child is devoid of pain? Each of our five children has caused us pain in his or her own way. I know my four eldest will forgive me if I say that Nicholas's tiniest achievements give me as much joy, if not more, than theirs did as babies, because he has taught us the supreme lesson: *take nothing for granted*, and rejoice in everything you can.

  1974

- Early in the morning of 12 September 1959 the phone rang. 'Please,' said the voice at the other end, 'will you foster a special baby for me? She may need to stay longer than usual, as she has a deformed face and is possibly a mongol. There are some feeding difficulties, a heart condition and. . . . Oh dear, the poor little scrap! Well, can I bring her this morning?'

  As I took baby Joy in my arms that morning there was a sense of love for the tiny little mite – I was sure she had come to stay. There was a hollow in her face just below the cheekbone, probably caused by pressure before birth, and she weighed just five pounds. The next few months were not easy. Feeding was a problem. She would gain a few ounces one week and lose them the next; each feed took over an hour and the baby seemed too tired to suck. At three and a half months old I decided to spoon-feed her with strained foods – despite the frowns of the health visitor, who thought she was much too tiny. Joy loved her new food, however, maintained a steady weight gain, and never looked back. At six months, it was confirmed that Joy was a Down's Syndrome baby. Her face no longer showed signs of the hollow; she was rather pretty and I was very proud of her. She loved listening to music and was very happy and contented. She sat up unaided for short periods by the time she was 14 months old, and made her way across the floor like a spider on her feet and hands at 18 months. When, on her second birthday, Joy took her first steps, we were all so overjoyed we sat watching her with tears running down our faces.

When she was three years old we were told that Joy was ineducable, and that arrangements had been made for her to attend the local school for mentally handicapped children. However, I did not think she was ready for school, and had quite a battle with the officials to keep her at home with me until she was toilet-trained. She achieved this by the time she was four-and-a-half, and was then able to go off confidently to school. When she was six the children at the school performed a Christmas play in a local theatre. It was 'The Sleeping Princess', and Joy was the good fairy. Because most of the children had speech difficulties it was all done in mime, but it was fantastic to see those children perform, they knew exactly what they were doing, and how they all enjoyed it! I went to every performance – I couldn't keep away.

It was after this I tried desperately to get speech therapy for Joy but I was unsuccessful. I was told that this possibility was only for normal children who would not speak. Fortunately, things are very different today. Now, 23 years old, Joy attends an adult training centre, but sadly her speech is very limited. She does, however, enjoy good health and is certainly a happy, loving and much loved member of the family.

1982

● Before the February 1979 PPIAS Newsletter arrived, we had

Adoption: the inside story

thought for a number of years that our family was complete, having two natural daughters then aged 16 and 15 years and two mixed-raced adopted sons, 11 and 9 years. On reading the Newsletter I was immediately drawn to a little girl named Barbara. She was nearly five, and quite severely disabled with spina bifida. She was paralysed from the waist down, doubly incontinent, and was only able to stand for a few minutes with the aid of callipers.

I told myself for a week or two what an impractical idea it was to enlarge the family, especially with a disabled child, but found I could not get her out of my thoughts. We discussed the possibility, and then rang her social worker. From there on things

Lucy with her adoptive parents, Janet and John, brothers Matthew (standing) and Julian, and sisters Philippa (standing) and Nichola.

seemed to move quite rapidly. Lucy (as she is now called) had spent almost her entire life in care, and the authorities were very keen to settle her with a family. Having completed the necessary preliminaries, and having made sure that the children were all in favour of an addition to the family, we set off to visit Lucy. That was the finish of any doubts. Once we had seen her there was no turning back. Many hundreds of miles were clocked up on the car over the next few months, as we started regular visits. Within a few weeks Lucy was visiting our home. She fitted in from the beginning, and the partings soon became traumatic for everyone.

On 10 July 1979 Lucy moved in with us, and we all had a period of adjusting to live through. Family life with a disabled child must inevitably call for a number of changes. Suddenly we were a lot more tied than we had been for a considerable time. Even a short trip to the shops was a lot more involved; it is not until you are in the position of shopping with a disabled person that you realise how inadequate the facilities are: lifts, ramps, toilets, parking etc. Life with a handicapped person also means a lot of extra work. Lucy's legs need exercising; she has to be encouraged to walk with her callipers and walking frame. We have to do regular physiotherapy exercises, and she needs help with most of the things a normal child can do unaided. Each year she is getting heavier to lift about, and we make regular trips to a London hospital for check-ups and tests.

Our reward has been to see her blossoming out, and to watch her achievements, however small. She has been accepted by other children in the neighbourhood and belongs to a number of local clubs. We are ambitious for her to become as independent as possible, and hope that she will grow up wanting to branch away on her own. One of the hardest things is to stop people over-compensating her, in the form of food and sweets, and also offering too much in the way of help. Bringing up any child is not always easy, but we feel that a lot of problems are only as big as you make them. Anyone who is considering adopting a handicapped child should think positively and go ahead. Lucy has obviously brought problems and anxieties when she has been ill, but the pleasures and joys far outweigh them.

1983

- Our son, Oliver, came to us by courtesy of the social services department of an inner London borough in November 1979, when he was just twelve weeks old. He was our first child. In March, after the statutory medical which pronounced him sound in mind and limb, he became ours, amid scenes of great rejoicing. At nine months he went for his first hearing test, to which he did not respond, but we weren't worried – we were sure that he was one of those babies who was 'visual' and not specially interested in spoon-in-cup noises! When he failed to respond to the health visitor twice more, she referred us to the audiology clinic, where the bomb was dropped – he seemed to be very deaf, we were told. A week later we saw the 'deaf doctor' who confirmed the diagnosis – profoundly deaf.

From that day, for about three weeks, I was in a state of shock, though mercifully my husband, Peter, remained calm and positive. We were helped by some good friends with experience of deafness who hastened to tell us that all deaf children in these days learn to speak. We were also advised to be referred to the Nuffield Centre in London, whose care and support has been magnificent – even including residential courses for the whole family, which gave us an opportunity to meet other mothers with young deaf children. A teacher of the deaf has visited us at home each week for two and a half years, and Oliver also goes to speech therapy most weeks. Peter and I are members of the National Deaf Children's Society and go to local meetings, where we meet other parents of deaf children and learn about aspects of deafness.

We knew that Oliver's disability could not have been diagnosed before he was adopted, and we have always been very grateful that there was no suspicion of it until after he was legally ours. It would have been an agonizing thing to have suspected before he was legally ours – but by four months afterwards there was no problem at all. He was as much a member of our family as if he had been born to us. In addition, we were in the enviable position of not having to feel guilty at having produced a deaf child. We would, of course, like to know what caused the deafness, but with only the information that we have about his parents and their antecedents it may not be possible.

Soon after his first birthday Oliver got his first hearing aid, and since then he has had two others. His progress has been remarkable, thanks to early detection, and now, at nearly four, he knows hundreds of words and can make himself understood in most situations. He doesn't yet string sentences together, but he has just now started at a school with a partially hearing unit, so we hope for great things! Previously he spent a happy year in a playgroup with normal hearing children. We hope that after a few years in the partially hearing unit he might be able to manage in a local school, but this will depend on the development of his speech.

Although there is nothing that can be done to improve Oliver's hearing, there have been some amazing technological advances in the three years since we discovered that he was deaf. At that time we were told he would never be able to wear post-aural hearing aids (ones that sit behind the ear with no wiring) because there were none powerful enough for his profound deafness, but by his third birthday he was wearing post-aurals with excellent results and, apart from his throwing one over the battlements at Windsor Castle and, on another occasion, swallowing a battery, they have been trouble-free and of great benefit to him! Another major recent development has been in the field of radio aids. These enable the input to a microphone near the speaker's mouth to be transmitted directly by radio waves to the hearing aid, so the deaf person can pick out a particular speaker from a confusing background noise, without having to look at him. We are in the process of buying one for Oliver and now, for the first time, I can attract his attention from far away and when he has his back to me. Finally, I would say, do consider adopting a deaf child. The majority of even profoundly deaf children are now able to learn to speak to a very acceptable degree; and with back-up from specialist doctors, teachers of the deaf, speech therapists and special schools, it is a challenge that, most of the time, is a pleasure to try to meet!

1983

- We adopted our son as a baby. He was placed with us at seven weeks old and we did not know until he was 14 months old that he was spastic, so we did not choose to adopt a handicapped child. Indeed, we felt that we were only capable of adopting a white, normal, healthy child (a view which at that time I am sure our social worker shared). We have, fortunately, all changed our minds in the last seven years.

I think initially the main difficulties of coping with the situation was the attitude of the medical staff, who thought that we were mad actually choosing (in their eyes) to keep a handicapped child. I can remember getting very upset and being very shocked at the attitude of medical staff and *some* social workers who just could not understand that we loved our son as if he had been born to us, and that our feelings were very similar to those of all other parents; and whilst other parents at the hospital and various groups I attended treated me normally until the subject of the birth difficulties came up, once they knew our son was adopted they too thought I was an oddity! However, those days are all behind us now, and we are more than grateful for all the help we have been given by the various therapists we have had during the past eight years.

Our son attends a school for the physically handicapped: he needs special education, as he would not cope educationally in a normal class. He does learn eventually, but it takes longer for him to grasp things. He has managed to walk unaided reasonably well in the last year, although he still needs a wheelchair for outdoor use; but he is one of the most mobile in the school, and he is finding it difficult to understand why he is (in his eyes) very mobile and yet cannot run or walk like everyone else. This is one of the problems with this sort of handicap where one is not wheelchair-bound, is within normal limits of intelligence, but is handicapped: the feeling of not quite fitting into either the world of the normal or the world of the handicapped.

I think the most physically exhausting and difficult part of coping as parents is that we have to try to help him to do normal things, which does mean a lot of lifting, etc. He has difficulties when he is out of doors playing, or at the playgrounds, when he wants to climb like everyone else, but his legs will not go with his body and sometimes will not even bend in the right place when pushed! However, even this is getting better, and we were overjoyed when, during the summer holidays, he had enough confidence to go to the small park a few doors from home with his sister – somehow between them he managed to get onto the swing and she pushed! (I watched from the kitchen window, in case I was needed!)

Having both a handicapped child and a 'normal' child does of course present problems, and we are becoming more aware as the children get older that they must each be catered for, and that we must not hold our daughter back because of our son's problems. We hope that he will enrich her life as indeed she does his.

In a nutshell – having a handicapped child is great, it is more rewarding (than with normal children) when goals are achieved. The joy of seeing a child walk (however badly) after years of striving is indescribable, the thrill of managing to put the first piece of a jig-saw in a hole after hours and hours of trying, the thrill of putting one brick on top of another. Living with handicap is also very demanding, tiring and frustrating; and although for us the joy of having our son outweighs the difficulties, I would advise anyone thinking of adopting an older handicapped child to be sure they can cope with the handicap, and can grow to love the child behind the disability.

This is a list of 'musts' for adoptive parents of handicapped children:

- Be able to accept life as it is.
- Laugh at situations when others might cry.
- Give until it hurts, even without response.
- Never give up even if you seem to be getting nowhere – leave it and try again later.
- Put the achievements before the failures and praise everything good.
- Do not worry about people's comments about adoption or handicap.
- Be able to be the odd one out without worrying about it.
- Do not be put off because your child cannot do everything other children his age can do.
- Encourage him/her *all* the time.
- Help him always to be able to accept himself as he is, and to cope with life as well as he can.
- Above all teach him to be able to love, because he has always to be given a lot of love. Even a severely handicapped child will respond to love, just like a tiny baby.
- Love your child always as if he had been born to you. Even if you do find something to blame in the natural background, don't think about it – let alone worry about it. It might have been far worse if he had been born to you and you were blaming your own family.
- Always treat him as normally as possible.
- Learn about your child as he learns. It's great, and you'll be able to help him better.
- Always be honest with him when he asks 'why?' The truth will hurt more if he isn't told until he is a teenager.
- Help your child to grow into a happy adult whatever his disability.
- Never be afraid to ask for help or explanation if you don't understand the situation.

- Never tire of repetition. A handicapped child goes through each stage of development but later than average and for a longer period – but it's great when he gets there!

1982

CHAPTER 3

Adopting babies

Many couples who discover that they are unable to have their own children turn to the idea of adopting. Fifteen to twenty years ago they would probably have found it fairly easy to be matched with the baby they longed for. Today, however, the situation is very different. Improved contraceptive methods and the easier availability of abortion have resulted in fewer unwanted babies being born. The social stigma attached to unmarried mothers has, on the whole, disappeared, with the result that many single women, who might previously have given up their babies for adoption nowadays feel encouraged to keep them. Healthy babies, then, are rarely available for adoption — but parents *are* still needed for babies with special needs. It may be that a childless couple will discover that they can satisfy their desire for parenthood by adopting a handicapped child. The last story in this chapter describes just such a case, but more than that, it will strike chords for many parents who have been fortunate enough to adopt a baby.

Three of the other families whose accounts are featured here are white families who adopted black or mixed-race babies at a time, about ten years ago, when such babies were hard to place, and transracial adoption, so essential if the child was to avoid a life in care, less controversial than it is today.

Together the five accounts touch upon most of the important aspects involved in baby adoption; and two which are written by fathers reflect what appears to be the current trend for fathers to take a more active and interested role in baby care than in the past.

- Our daughter was placed with us when she was ten days old. The first we heard of her was two days before, when our social worker telephoned to say she had been born and would we like to go and see her. We were flung into parenthood summarily, without warning.

During the past year we had gone through the vetting process, which was itself a harrowing experience, arousing in us all kinds of self-doubts and fears. It dominated our lives at the time, making us feel angry, worried, confused, and making us wonder how on earth anyone could tell whether we would make suitable parents or not. We had many interviews, but could never tell what the social worker thought about us, or whether in fact she was on our side, and the end result was that we felt demoralized and unhappy. These feelings were, of course, completely wiped out when we were told that we had been approved, and we swung to the other extreme of euphoria and confidence, rather as if we had passed our finals. After that we settled down for a long wait, which was a boring prospect, but at least was free of all the worrying attention that had bedevilled us during the previous months.

Strangely enough, this freedom continued after our baby was placed with us, in that apart, from one visit and a couple of telephone calls, our social worker did not contact us. After such an exhaustive process to determine whether or not we were fit to have a child, it seemed odd to us at the time that some support was not considered necessary, particularly as we had had but two days to change our roles, from being simply man and wife, to being parents and child. In fact, we received marvellous support from our friends, relatives and neighbours, and I was rarely alone during those first weeks with the baby. The health visitor was a tower of strength, calling round (by appointment always, so I never felt I was being checked up on) and ringing up in between. I was made to feel that I could ring her at any time over the smallest worry, and baby and I were warmly welcomed at the clinic.

Looking back, I wonder rather sadly whether I would have welcomed 'support' from our social worker. At the time, although approved, we were still smarting from the effects of the search and probing interviews, and I think I would have been too distrustful to have accepted help from someone whom I had experienced at times as being quite inhibiting. In a way, the health visitor was neutral and gave us support in an extremely unbiased way, her only interest being that a new mother and her baby should have the best possible start together in both practical and emotional terms.

All new parents suffer from feelings of inadequacy, but adoptive parents perhaps have a greater need for support to restore their confidence and self-esteem during the early days of adjustment to sudden parenthoood.

1979

- As a father I had experienced the excitement of the birth of our first two children. I was, however, aware of a very different emotional involvement at an early stage, with our third child, an adopted daughter who arrived as a tiny four-week-old infant. The first two children had already developed a strong relationship with my wife during nine months of pregnancy, labour and the first days of handling in hospital. I felt a respect for that special bond between mother and child, and it took a little time before I was able to overcome the feeling of intrusion and begin to make my own contacts which naturally developed into a deep relationship and love for my children.

  It was a secretly thrilling experience to discover that when our adopted baby was handed to us, I was starting a new parent relationship on the same footing as my wife. There is little doubt that I became more involved with this child in the first days than I had with the others, was anxious to share in her caring, feeding, nursing, and was up at her first cry in the night. Both mother and father relationships were developing simultaneously. I have had the opportunity of meeting quite a number of adoptive families and have noticed how often the fathers are the ones carrying the new baby, whereas normally, I feel, mothers assume the carrying role of the child they have recently given birth to. I believe adoption has one small bonus for fathers!

1979

- Before we were offered a baby, my main worry was whether I'd love it enough, or even at all. When I confessed this to natural mothers, they said they'd felt the same before their babies were born and in some cases didn't really take to their offspring for days, or even weeks, after the birth. But our situation would be different, I thought: we might have absolutely nothing in common with the mixed-race baby we'd opted for. And so it turned out. The boy we were offered – we'd wanted a girl – was pure Indian. I went trembling to the hospital to see him, having been told he was 'all hair and nose'. Sure enough, he was (the nurses called him 'loo brush', which we were meant to be amused by), as well as having great eyes that rolled back to show nothing but the whites and a totally austere expression. Poor thing, he'd been in the premature unit for six weeks. When I visited him at the foster mother's I gradually grew accustomed to his face, but I didn't love it. Undoubtedly I'd have bonded more quickly if he'd looked more like a conventional baby, more like my nephew and nieces in fact. My husband, who had no experience of babies but positive feelings about Indians, responded immediately and saw him for what he was, a defenceless, extremely distressed tiny human. What made me love him finally was emerging from the bad times (he cried almost unceasingly for his first five days with us) into the good, and finding we had a baby who laughed readily as well as smiled. Going through the motions of caring undoubtedly helped too, as well as the warm support of family and friends. It was only when I met people who looked askance at interracial adoption or adoption at all, that I felt the cold hand of alienation and wondered what I was doing sitting with someone else's baby on my knee. But as the months went by he felt like our baby, and now he feels like our lovely son, still not much like us and not altogether easy, but nevertheless inextricably ours.

1982

- Our daughter, Anna, was adopted as a baby, and is now seven. Though the placing agency presumably did 'assess' us, we never felt under scrutiny, but were asked to write about our relationships with our parents and each other. We had two children, attempted to find a baby with mixed racial origins, with or without a physical handicap, and after 29 false starts found a small agency in a very 'white' town looking for a family who had specifically wanted a mixed-race baby. The natural mother wanted existing children in the adoptive family, and our form luckily fitted the social worker's request of BAAF Newcastle, our thirtieth attempt.

    Throughout visits by us to the agency (where our four- and two-year-olds were riotously disruptive and the social worker made positive comments about extrovert children), and visits by the social worker to our small, childworn home, we felt the social worker was being accepting and encouraging, and we were in fact accepted to adopt despite the agency's case committee's incredulity that a fertile couple would want to adopt!

Anna arrived four weeks premature, and the social worker was happy for me to visit daily until Anna was discharged from hospital. The value of those brief visits to me was immense, and I hope made the move home less traumatic for Anna. I had hoped to breastfeed Anna (I had the first two children), though re-lactating was something we had initially planned to keep secret lest we be thought freaks! However, our social worker was predictably accepting, and genuinely enthusiastic, when I talked to her about it. Placing Anna direct from hospital made feeding, and settling in generally, far easier and quicker – *well* worth the risk to us of losing Anna before six weeks. All the recent work of people like Leboyer must surely help the first weeks of a baby's life to be seen as too crucial to bonding to justify short-term fostering except when absolutely necessary?

Our social worker enthusiastically agreed to Anna's natural mother's request to meet us all. She saw such meetings as potentially helpful in many, though of course not in all, adoptions. Anna's 'first mother' had wanted to see Anna as part of her adopted family, and be reassured that some early medical problems had been resolved. We have since found the meeting invaluable, when telling Anna about her 'first mother', though it was of course traumatic for everyone at the time.

With hindsight we realise how very fortunate we were, not only in finding Anna, but also in having a reassuring social worker and hospital visits before placement, and in meeting Anna's 'first mother', which all helped so much.

1984

- We rose at 7 am on Wednesday, 21 April 1982. By 'we' I mean my wife, Julie, and myself. We sat in silence whilst we pondered on what the next 24 hours would bring. The previous evening we had spent getting everything 'ship shape', going from top to bottom with the vacuum cleaner, polishing furniture and generally tidying up, especially the room that until today we had always called 'the spare room'. What was the reason for all this excitement and hard work? Today Julie and I were to become parents for the first time.

OK, we all know people who have become parents for the first time, but this is different. We know it is going to be today: the baby won't be early, it won't be late; we know what sex it is going to be. I'm not walking up and down chain smoking in some maternity hospital, Julie isn't in hospital, she's not even pregnant. She hasn't had nine months of morning sickness, cravings for jellied eels and ice cream, no ultrasound scans, high blood-pressure and the like. No, we are both sitting calmly drinking our morning cup of tea, knowing that at 11 am we are picking up our very own baby girl. Of course, you've guessed it: today we are going to adopt an eight-month-old baby.

All right, let's throw in this paragraph of official jargon so as not to upset the social services department. From today we are to become foster parents to a baby girl. We will receive the boarding out allowance, then after 13 weeks or so we apply to adopt, then after 20 weeks or so it goes to court for our application to be considered, etc. etc. But as far as we are concerned, from today she is our little girl; after all, when all the adoption papers have come through we are not going to turn to our little girl and say, 'From tomorrow fortnight you are ours.' We are not going to wake up that morning and feel any different from the day before, whereas in 24 hours from now things are certainly going to be different.

Our biggest worry is whether she will sleep OK. After all she has never slept here before, strange cot, strange bedroom, strange house; but at least we won't seem strange to her – thanks to the cooperation of the foster mother, we have seen an awful lot of Karen (that's the name we have decided to give her) over the past four weeks. Funnily enough, it has taken almost exactly nine months to get our little Karen. Nine months, that is, since our first interview with the social workers, the first of a series of interviews with a view to adopting. We both came through our medicals all right, and by mid-October 1981 we were approved as prospective adoptive parents. Then, nothing for about four months until early one Saturday morning, and right out of the blue, we got a telephone call: 'We may have a baby for you.' From that moment on our lives became totally different.

Apart from today, our most important day was when we went to visit our baby for the first time. We were taken by a social worker to the foster mother's flat to have a look at a baby in order to decide whether or not we would like her for our own, an incredible decision to have to make. Admittedly we didn't have to decide there and then. We had already discussed it and knew before we went that we need not choose the first baby that we saw. It's a strange sensation almost to have the power over this baby's destiny, in theory anyway, to be able to say, 'No, we don't like this one. What else have you got on the shelf?' It almost sounds cruel, but if one is to devote one's life to the upbringing of this child, then one has to be absolutely sure, and

I use the words 'devote one's life' carefully, as the child we are going to adopt is a Down's Syndrome child. In the event, as soon as we saw this baby we both knew that she was the one for us. The fact that we were both so sure was very lucky for us - and I hope for the baby. I am convinced that had the baby not been to our immediate liking we would have had no hesitation in saying, 'We don't feel we could share our lives with this child.' Having made this important decision, we spent the next four weeks paying visits to the foster mother's home. This is where the second piece of luck came in because Julie, I and the foster mother all got on very all together. The foster mother was extremely helpful, and was to prove a vital factor in the following four weeks of getting to know our new arrival. Over the four-week period we spent about 14 days with Karen, either at the foster mother's home or our own, and Karen seemed to take to us just as we had to her.

So it's 11 am, 21 April, and we pick up Karen and the foster mother and take them back to our home. There we open a bottle of champagne as a token of our celebration. A social worker arrives at 2 pm and we sign the relevant papers; the only slight disappointment is that the child has to retain her own name for the time being, but we shall call her Karen, of course. The social worker and foster mother depart and we spent the rest of the afternoon playing with Karen. Up until 6 pm it seems the same as the other 14 days we have spent with her. By 8 pm she has her last feed, and it's coming up to the big testing time. Will she sleep OK? I rig up the baby alarm and Julie puts her in her cot. Lo and behold, she goes to sleep almost immediately. It's 8.30 pm and we switch on the television and half-heartedly watch the comparatively unimportant news of the Falklands crisis, whilst at the same time we make regular visits to the baby's bedroom to check that the baby alarm is working. One of us breathes into the microphone to see if the other partner can hear it. Of course, in actual fact you can even hear Karen breathing. Julie and I retire about midnight and we lie in bed waiting for Karen to wake up. I mean, she's bound to, isn't she? We turn out the light and go to sleep. But neither of us sleeps well - I myself wake up several times, and each times I do Julie is already awake, but Karen - no way. Our alarm goes off at 7 am. We both get up and peer into Karen's room - shhh, she's still asleep. By 7.45 I leave for work, Julie is busy making up bottles. And Karen? She's still asleep, of course.

1983

CHAPTER 4

The terrible twos: adopting toddlers

Toddlers are contrary creatures as a rule, struggling to be assertive and independent on the one hand yet fearful of separation from their mothers on the other. Children whose lives are 'interrupted' during this time by being moved from one set of parents or caretakers to another are not likely to have an easy passage through this crucial stage of their development: their need to assert themselves may be exhibited in more frequent and aggressive tantrums than are usual in a toddler, their fear of separation by even more clingy behaviour than is the norm. Some children whose lives are disrupted when they are toddlers may still be working through this stage when they are much, much older. A couple thinking of adopting a child in 'the terrible twos' need to have not only an enormous amount of patience and energy, but also, more importantly, the ability to love, no matter what happens, and to give that love, at least at first, without expecting any in return. If they can do this, according to the families who share their experiences with us in this chapter, there *are* rewards to be reaped in the end.

The terrible twos: adopting toddlers

- Wayne had had his second birthday and farewell party at the children's home the day before he came to us. I think Melanie, our rather dainty little girl, was upset by his size, although I had explained he was not a baby. She still expected someone who would fit into some baby boots she had found in a drawer, not someone who could wear her four-year-old shoes with ease.

  It would be easy with natural pride to gloss over the last year and say that these past months were what we expected, but in honesty, they have been far, far worse. Wayne has pulled out all the stops in his settling down period. He has had many tantrums in a variety of places, ranging from the fish and chip shop to the public library. During these tantrums he will screech, kick, throw things, bite and be sick (not so good in the public library). These tantrums can last from 30 minutes to one hour and are exhausting, for both him and us. It has also been very difficult to mix with other children of Wayne's age, as he constantly has to be stopped knocking other children about. With the best will in the world, it is hard for other mothers to watch their offspring being beaten over the head by this large brown-skinned child. (They are so eager not to be prejudiced that they find it hard to chastise him without feeling that we will take it as a sign of deeper dislike.) Melanie and Ashley, however, have stuck by him through thick and thin, and he has grown to enjoy their company enormously; and there are most definitely many more smiles than there were a year ago!

  The most rewarding thing is that at last he now holds up his arms to be loved and comforted. When he came to us he would only kick and bite if we tried to show affection. It is also lovely that he can now run to us for a 'kiss it please' when he falls over. His previous reaction was to curl up in a small heap without crying, and rock to and fro on the floor.

  I think the thing *we* have had to learn is that no matter how much love we had to give, it was an unknown quality to Wayne, and he found it hard to accept all at once. After all, it must take a long time to get over being 'nobody's child'.

1973

- Michael took a long time to unwind and be himself in his new home – which was to be expected after nine months in a large children's home, a kind of interlude between us and the first two, very unhappy, years of his life. For about three months we felt as if we had a small, polite visitor in the house, but that period ended as some of the real difficulties worked their way to the surface. Michael was endlessly proud of us, his new parents, (although 'Mummy' was a word he rejected completely) but he also suffered intense anxiety lest someone would come to take him away. Things were not made any easier by the many visits from different social workers concerned with Michael's case – they stirred up his unease.

There were times when Michael was indeed a very unhappy little boy, yet it was always possible to point to some area in which he was making progress. He soon made friends with children his own age in the village – this despite his strong cockney accent, a slight speech defect and a very limited vocabulary! But we all suffered from his exhausting temper tantrums, and for four weeks or more he wouldn't go out of the house, not even into the garden to play. Going out anywhere always produced symptoms of anxiety, unidentified aches and pains, or awkward demands and sulks. Our first family holiday, to stay in Granny's house by the sea, was anything *but* a holiday for us. But it was worth it, to see Michael's delight when we came home again – yes, it really *was* home. Another major problem was nightmares – every night, for perhaps 18 months, Michael would wake up screaming, not once in the night, but often twice.

If I seem to have dwelt on our difficulties, well, making an older child feel at home isn't easy, the more so if that child has suffered at other people's hands. As would-be parents you need patience and understanding, and time. I write this almost three and a half years after Michael first arrived, and we have watched him grow into a happy, confident little boy. He loves visitors, and going visiting, has a bike and rides it anywhere in the village, thinks school is smashing, and in private admits to being 'super-boy'. What more reward could we want?

1973

- Our social worker described Claire as a stocky, strong-willed toddler of mixed-race parentage, aged two-and-a-half. To our disappointment, she was living in a children's home in the north of England, and we had to content ourselves for a few days with three black and white photographs and some biographical details. The photos suggested she was a tough little person, and the biographical details suggested she had needed to be. I went to see her at the earliest possible moment.

The first meeting was disappointing. She had a very bad cold and a touch of bronchitis, was unfriendly, grumpy and weepy, and not at all interested in me or any of the books or toys I tried to interest her in. She could speak only a few words, and seemed to understand very little that I said to her. I was allowed to bath her in the evening – a frustrating experience, since she would not let me touch her or anything that belonged to her. The next morning I took her for a walk after breakfast, keeping up an animated monologue about dogs, birds, cars, during which her solemn, suspicious gaze never left my face. There had been talk of ten successive weekend visits before a trial placement, so we were amazed when we returned as a family the next weekend and were told that because of various problems in the children's home we could take her home at once (complete with social worker, who quite fancied a weekend in London). It had been only a week since we first heard of her, and we were quite definitely unprepared for the storms to follow. Claire was, we now realize, at about the worst possible time developmentally, being right in the middle of 'the terrible twos'. With her strong and independent personality, I can imagine she would have been a handful at this age with the most normal of upbringings. She had, however, had a very neglected infancy, and had just been removed abruptly from the only home and stable mother-figures she had ever known, to live with complete strangers who talked with strange southern accents and looked as if they knew they weren't coping too well.

She was very brave under the circumstances, but obviously very disturbed. She barely ate, spent long periods crying or sitting doing absolutely nothing, and would not let me out of her sight (although she took many months to forgive me for not being her house mother).

1979

- Our little foster daughter arrived two days before her second birthday, having spent the previous month in hospital, where she was admitted with injuries thought to have been inflicted by her mother's cohabitee. She is a very resilient little person and adjusted to our large (and noisy) family and all the coming and goings involved, with good humour. She observed it all with wide eyes and fingers firmly placed in her mouth for comfort.

At first, every time we left the house she would go quiet and tense, and then on our return she would rush round happily with an obvious release of tension. Getting into the car involved all the children piling in first and then my bags being put carefully in so that she knew I was coming too; only then would she let me lift her in to sit happily cuddled by one of the children. The other very marked worry for her was that we allowed – and even encouraged – her to get mucky during play activities. The first time water play was set up she howled guiltily when some was spilt. Sand is still regarded with suspicion and brushed hastily off her hands. Similar reactions occurred if food was dropped – although watching the rest of the family eating has no doubt helped her to overcome this!

I think our biggest problem is to prevent her new brother and sisters from 'spoiling' her. Having established her place in the family she regards everything in the house as 'hers', and needs help to accept that she can safely share it all with little playmates.

1979

- Having very painlessly adopted a four-month-old, mixed-race baby boy to join our two naturally born girls, we felt able and keen to add an older child to round off the family. While we knew there would be difficulties with a child who had spent two and a half years in care, we felt that our knowledge that we could take someone else's child would be a great advantage to us. The children we already had were very enthusiastic about our having another brother, and were not worried about his not being a baby. Everything seemed adequately prepared. Indeed, from the children's point of view this was the case. Being so concerned with how everyone else was going to manage the new relationship, I didn't prepare myself for the emotional problems that *I* was going to experience.

Paul had been through a difficult first two years. He spent six months with his mother, who was not able to cope and left him alone at night, so that when he went into care he was a very tense baby with a well established sleep and crying problem. He went to a residential nursery and stayed there for a year. A foster home placement followed, but this only lasted six months and he went back to the nursery. His hyperactive behaviour and very disturbing nights were too much for the experienced foster parents, and tranquillizers did not calm him down. A decision to close the nursery revealed that it was most unlikely that Paul's mother would ever provide a home for him, and so adoption was planned. We met him after he had been back in the nursery for six months, obviously still suffering from the rejection by the foster parents. He was assessed as depressed, was on tranquillizers again and was having one illness after another. A proper little hypochondriac we went to meet! We were very concerned by the report of his behaviour and poor sleeping, but decided we could cope. He sounded such a bright little boy, so we went to see him and the commitment was made. The first months we had him remain a memory of just coping. We weaned him off his drug without too much difficulty, and the other children were marvellous in their tolerance of his enormous demands and antisocial behaviour. One day I calculated an average of one tantrum every 20 minutes!

It was when people around us were commenting on what a big improvement there was in him and how marvellous we were that I found that I began to question my ability to accept him. There is little doubt that ours was an arranged marriage that I would not have entered under normal circumstances. I felt very resentful that his demands made such an emotional hole in me, and I could see that the other children were losing out on attention. This was particularly true of Peter, now rising five and starting school. I think that the acknowledgement to myself that Paul was a menace, and that I didn't love him as much as the others, in some way helped me to turn the corner. Had I not had the strong sense of commitment to him, which was made before we really knew him, I think I would have given up. A further complication was that the adoption hearing was contested by his natural mother and the outcome was by no means certain. We won the case nearly a year ago, and life has steadily improved.

I can now begin to see the situation more clearly and the rewards are beginning to show. Paul is still a menace but is contributing to family life, and I am more able to see the wood, not the trees. I can see his personality traits as individual to himself and providing variety within the family, rather than threatening to my own security and even sanity! The experience has matured me, I am sure. I know now that it is important not to think too hard under stress but to let things evolve. Had we fostered Paul I am sure that he would not be with us now. The commitment I had made was the challenge which said, 'I will not be beaten.' My husband, through all this, managed to cope with the problems of the hour, although it was he who initially had the greater misgivings. Paul goes to nursery school, where he is disruptive but improving; he has grown up a lot and learned to swim! Since the end of the tranquillizers he has only seen a doctor to have his adoption medical, and I am able to be truthful when I say that his coming has been of benefit to all of us. I might even recommend the experience to someone else – cautiously of course!

CHAPTER 5

The turbulent teens: adopting teenagers

One of the most difficult times to adopt or foster a child must be during his adolescence. This is a stage of life when children should, and do, seek independence from the family. How then can they be expected to form new family attachments at this time?

Couples thinking of taking on a teenager need to be able to provide the right amount of security for him and, at the same time, be able to judge when and how to give him scope to break away and be responsible for himself. Involving their teenager in making decisions about family matters may help to develop his sense of responsibility and show to him that he is an equal partner in the relationship. At least he is more likely to be cooperative if he has some say in what standards are set, and what punishments and rewards there are to be had!

The teenager's new parents should expect to be tested too. They may have to face problems usually associated with a much younger child. Their teenager may have difficulty in living up to the expectations of others; he may perform poorly at school, be lacking in social skills, and find difficulty in articulating his feelings. His new family will have to be prepared to help him sort out and work through the sad parts of his *earlier* life at a stage when most young people are trying to establish their identity in an *adult* world.

Taking a teenager is definitely not an easy task! In this chapter four families describe how they coped, what made them feel like giving up and what kept them going! Finally, Phillida Sawbridge, Director of Parents for Children, who has enormous experience of introducing older children into new families, gives some helpful advice on what to consider before adopting or fostering a teenager.

The turbulent teens: adopting teenagers

- Having been in care since the age of ten months, John came to us two months after his twelfth birthday. Early attempts to place him in foster homes had failed, largely due to his inability to give or receive affection, and he had spent six years in a children's home, during which time he had had four different sets of house parents. Backward in his school work, not so much from lack of ability as from lack of any motivation to work or even to take an interest, and a square peg in the round hole of a large London comprehensive, it looked as if he would end up in a special school when we came on the scene. We still have the feeling that we were a last ditch, and there have been many times when we have felt that way. We were told as much of his background as was known, but it wasn't much (we still don't know if he has had measles!), including that he had stolen money more than once and was emotionally withdrawn. We were given various reports of the different attempts to place him over the years – these were suitably horrifying, but we felt it was all in the past and we must take it on day-to-day basis.

After a fortnight's holiday with us and a return trip to London to pack, John settled in with what seemed remarkable ease to start with. He liked his new school, made friends (a few of whom proved a bad influence), took a willing part in our church activities, and raced round the district on his bicycle. We began with the clear commitment to a permanent arrangement. John called us Mum and Dad from the beginning, took our surname, knew this was 'for keeps', and enjoyed his new grandparents most of all.

We had been warned that the testing time was after the first six months – and it was! We found he was stealing, first from us, then from other members of the family, from shops and school; only then did we learn from his social aunt and uncle that he had been stealing from them since he was five, but that they had just accepted it and made allowances. We dealt with it very severely, in addition to which he paid back every penny we knew about, but undoubtedly got away with some. More difficult was our lack of relationship with him. We felt he looked upon us as merely giving him a place to live – he liked it better than London because there wasn't so much traffic; if we'd sent him back he would just have shrugged and gone. It was like having a stranger in the house, who contributed nothing, said very little and cared for no-one, least of all himself.

The arrival of a West Indian sister aged four helped us to make a little more contact with John, as he saw himself more as one of the grown-ups in her world. Like all brothers and sisters, they quarrel, but John is mostly very good with her, and we think she may have roused the first spark of affection from him. A serious crisis developed soon after his fourteenth birthday. Coincidentally, a friend who had been in a foster home for over three years was sent back into care, making us all think about a possible escape from a seemingly permanently unhappy family life. As with other issues, we tried to talk the situation over with John, putting his future into his own hands, and eventually he said, 'I wanna stay.' So we have all been working to develop the necessary relationship, explaining yet again that belonging to a family means more than just living in the same house, and feeling that this time the explanation meant something.

In the last two months we have begun to see some encouragement – he has been more open and communicative, and we believe it is quite a long time since he stole anything. Now that his behaviour is controlled he has more freedom and the necessary structure in which to create full relationships, and we believe that only after a commitment has been established and a code of conduct accepted do these relationships have the possibility of maturing. We do not believe that sympathy and understanding are any substitute for discipline – the adult world will not take the line 'he didn't know any better' indefinitely – and anyway he *does* know now. We expect setbacks, but we also have hopes that the general direction will be forwards rather than backwards.

1974

- It is now almost a year since Ivor, a 14-year-old, joined our family of four adopted children, and eight months since Bruce, his elder brother of 16 years, came. So many things have happened in these months that it is difficult to give an adequate insight into the real depths of joy, frustration, fear, and physical, emotional and mental exhaustion that we experienced. Although we had been foster parents for 12 years and thought we knew it all, we very quickly learned just how inadequate we were going to feel with these two very disturbed boys. Their social worker had prepared us for their coming very well, but it was very different convincing her that we could deal with 'anything' and then experiencing the full ferocity of their anger against the society who had let them down.

As their foster mum, one thing I had to learn at top speed was that under no circumstances must I fail them in any way. After having spent most of their life in an institutionalized setting with an abundance of staff to cater to their every whim 24 hours a day, they felt very let down if we were not physically able to do the work of four people. If they felt like chicken and chips at 1 am in the morning, then they took it as their right that I would get up and cook it, and if I did not happen to have chicken in the house, then their pent-up aggression really came into force, and the verbal abuse that was thrown at us was indescribable. Many times I have stood in the kitchen in a cold sweat, hoping that my husband would be able to control Ivor and calm him down. The bionic woman had nothing on me – I was even accused of failing to *know in advance* what Ivor wanted for his tea. Meals with Ivor were a particular problem; he went through a stage of eating nothing but mushrooms for weeks on end; any attempt to get something else inside him was met with verbal aggression. We also had bedwetting problems – it's hard to cope with this problem in any child, but in a 15-year-old who flatly refuses to have a waterproof sheet in his bed it's really quite a task. Bruce was quite different – in fact the opposite – he said very little and suffered from bouts of depression. One day he would be quite pleasant, and the next day you would just get a grunt and be made to feel that you were the cause of his depression. Bruce also had eating problems; for several weeks he insisted on eating steak and kidney pie with chips and beans at every meal-time.

Yes, those first few months were a nightmare. Looking back now, we wonder how we coped, but amazingly we are still together. We now enjoy one another's company, our home is more settled. Ivor's aggression is now more controlled; any failure on our part is now greeted by a big 'Oh' and no verbal abuse. Their eating habits are the same as ours, and at normal meal-times. The bedwetting has now stopped, the depressions are nonexistent. Bruce is now happily settled in a job. Ivor is settled into school, and works part-time at a garage. Physically both have changed: they have grown several inches; and those two surly faces have become very relaxed, with a ready smile.

When we first met it wasn't love at first sight, but day by day we have got to know one another. We love our 'new sons' more today than yesterday, more this week than last week, and so we hope our relationship will go on steadily progressing into the future as they become more integrated members of our family. Was it really worth going through those first terrible months? We would say yes, most emphatically, especially when we heard Bruce thank his social worker for all she had done for him.

1979

- Having been approved as adoptive parents for two children aged between six and 11, we received, out of the blue, a telephone call from our social worker asking if we would be prepared to foster a girl of 15. We had to decide quickly, as Christine required a new home within a week. We decided to meet her and see if there was any reaction between us, in the knowledge that the normal lengthy introduction period would have to be dispensed with and a decision made on the spot; fortunately all went well at the introductory meeting. After 15 years of married life, with simply the two of us just pleasing ourselves what we did and when, we were suddenly faced with the prospect of family life and all that it would entail. Therefore, with some trepidation we collected Christine and embarked into the unknown.

Although 15, Christine was somewhat immature, with no real experience of a stable family life. She settled in fairly well at the beginning, possibly helped by the fact that she was able to return to the school where she had been prior to being taken into care. The school staff were good at helping her to resettle. Her attendance record had been very poor and she needed a lot of hard work to catch up with the syllabus before taking O levels the following year. The only problem she encountered at school was the fact that her friends found it difficult to adjust to the 'new' Christine, smartly dressed and attending punctually every day.

She took a long time to adjust completely to family life, and had difficulty in understanding that we were her parents. We were upset when, on the first two occasions she encountered personal problems, she headed for the local social services office seeking help. We told her that in future we wanted her to discuss her problems with us in family environment, as we were always there to help her with her problems, large or small. She finally understood this, and explained that she had never had anyone at home to turn to in the past. In the early days she also wanted to 'do her own thing' and go out with friends, regardless of what we might have planned to do within the family. Eventually matters were brought to a head when we firmly told Christine that if she intended to stay with us it would either be as an integral part of the family or as lodger. She opted for the family, and has not looked back since. Although the argument was unpleasant at the time, the desired result was achieved.

We took great pleasure in helping Christine with her school work, and were rewarded by her obtaining a place at the local college of further education, where she is now following a secretarial course and getting very good results. She has made rapid strides, and is now quite a sophisticated 17-year-old, well able to conduct herself in any company and able to hold an intelligent conversation.

We feel we are now a very settled family, and that we are lucky to have a good daughter, happy to do her share of the family chores and always cheerful and willing. We have derived great satisfaction from knowing that we have been instrumental in giving Christine a good start in life, and she has repaid us by being a very loving daughter.

1979

- We were not looking for a fifth child, but realizing that we had room and probably enough energy, it occurred to us that we could offer a teenager the experience of family life for the last two or three years in care. I really believe that fate produced the right child for us, a girl of nearly 16 who was very much in need of parenting, and so anxious to become part of our family that she called us 'Mummy' and 'Daddy' from the day she came to live with us. We never imagined that we would get such enormous returns from her so quickly – watching her gain confidence, begin to work with interest at school and to build real relationships with us all, has been very rewarding. At a time when most teenagers are rebelling and cutting free from parental ties, it is a pleasure to find that our new daughter is happy to spend evenings, weekends and holidays with us and her much younger sisters. Any worries we might have had over how we would handle late nights, boyfriends and uncertainties about where she might be have, so far, not come our way. On the other hand it is encouraging to see her interests widen as she becomes less dependent on television and pop radio.

Of course there have been days of irritation and worry, but no more than one would expect from any teenager, and I have been determined to keep my tolerance level high by constantly reminding myself that our older children, nieces or friends' children had the same sorts of problems – often worse! The initial minor, and probably inevitable, deceptions, which undermined our trust in the early days, I found the most difficult new ingredient in our family life. Nothing is worse than the sinking feeling of suspicion, the gruesome business of looking for proof and often the guilt of finding one was wrong. Fortunately, we hope those days are over.

1979

Adoption: the inside story

The Crawford children: Adam and Cleo (standing) and, from left to right, Lyndsay, Olivia and Suzy. (See also Chapters 3, 'Adopting babies', 6, 'Changing places', and 8, 'Bonding'.)

The turbulent teens: adopting teenagers

- The advertisement in the PPIAS Newsletter said; 'Peter will soon be 13, a cheerful, cheeky boy who is popular with adults and children. He loves to read, ... is affectionate and appreciative... would like to live with sporty, clever people who will help me with my homework and do interesting outdoor things.' We read it and looked at the photograph, and thought that maybe Peter would be happy in our family; youngish, teacher parents and adopted, half-West Indian three- and one-year-olds, living in the country. We expected an energetic teenager who was being held back by life in a children's home, and would blossom with love and attention from a family. Looking back, we feel that Peter and his social worker described the kind of child he thought would appeal to parents – it worked, and 18 months later he is still with us. In fact, although superficially cheerful, he is a deeply sad boy, too insecure to be cheeky or show any real emotion. He was unenergetic to the point of lethargy, and still needs encouragement to open any sort of book, and as for help with homework...! The fact that we expect him to do it at all is a constant bone of contention.

We expected all sorts of problems from a frustrated teenager, swearing, violence, stealing, bedwetting. We had the bedwetting, but that is improving. All our other problems have been far more negative than we expected. His insecurity meant that for the first year he spent nearly all of his nonschool time with us, even following me round the house to the lavatory, and watching me for hours in the kitchen. When a new friend in the village asked him out to play, his reply was, 'I'd rather be with the family.' A touching and telling remark, but for us it was stifling and irritating. The greatest improvement to his and our happiness has been his finding a gang of close friends this summer.

For my husband, one of the great disappointments has been the lack of interest he has taken in the world about him, and feeling that the stimulating life we have offered him has, to a large extent, passed him by unnoticed, from car-mending to camping in the mountains of Norway. It is a sad contrast (and a depressing reflection on the importance of stimulation early on in life) with our two younger children, whose intellectual energy, and capacity for absorbing and enjoying their surroundings, is amazing. One of my major irritations is being treated as a permanent and never off-duty member of staff, whose job it is to pick up dirty socks, remove cowmuck from carpets, etc. It has at last got through to him that if you go bicycling in your best trousers, and tear them, they will be patched rather than replaced. What a pity money in children's homes isn't spent as carefully as it is in a real home. During the last year he has lost seven pairs of trainer shoes, at least three sets of PE equipment, half a tracksuit, a leather jacket, and a £100 oboe (left at a bus stop). Of course all teenagers lose things, but we feel that this record is fairly extreme!

What has made all the difficulties bearable has been the relationship between Peter and our younger children. Since one weekend early on, when he tried to get between us and our three-year-old, and very speedily realized the position was unassailable, he has been as gentle, patient and loving a brother as you could imagine. He accepts their lavish doses of love and rough-and-tumble, and seems to benefit enormously from all the hero-worship and cuddles.

Far from swearing and bad manners, Peter is extremely well behaved. We have been able to rely on him to behave impeccably, for example, at recent family weddings, where we received all sorts of compliments on his appearance and behaviour. It has certainly made our life easier. His manners and obvious enjoyment of family get-togethers have smoothed his own path to acceptance by relations and friends. What changes have we seen in the last 18 months? He is still an insecure and undemonstrative person. It's hard to tell how much we mean to him. We know he likes life here – one of his friends told us that he said, 'It's like being on holiday all the time!' He has grown six inches, and is slim and browner and far more active. At school he is still pretty backward, but he is making progress.

It's hard work suddenly being parents to a teenager. The feedback is very small – no hugs, kisses, or 'it's nice living with you!' That's too much to expect from a child to whom so little has been given. We'd like him to call us 'Mum' and 'Dad' but we don't think he ever will. For us it's been an extraordinary time, full of interest and frustration. We don't look back, we'd never let him go, and we've never wavered in our decision, but we certainly feel we underestimated the difficulties.

1980

- Take in a teenager! You will be offering a highly prized service, but don't expect it to be like fostering or adopting a younger child. If you accept how different it is, you may be equipped to avoid some of the pitfalls. Here are some thinking-points:

Decision-making
Teenagers in care vary in the extent to which they have been allowed or are able to begin making decisions. Usually this is an area in which they are immature for their age. Some attend their own six-monthly reviews, many do not. Some have begun to learn to handle their own clothing allowance, decide minor matters for themselves – many have not. It will be important to discover what responsibilities your teenager has carried, and to take it on from there. With some, you will be starting from scratch, and you may feel you are dealing with a much younger child. But he or she is still 15 or 16 or whatever age it is, and sensitive about being treated as such.

Supports
If the teenager has had doubts about coming – and which of them won't have? – you too will have occasional doubts about your sanity in undertaking this thing. You will need support – however independent you usually are. Make sure your and/or the youngster's social worker arranges regular visits – better too many appointments which can be cancelled if not needed, than not to have the support when you need it. Find out when you can reach the social worker on the telephone. Find out what other adoptive parents of teenagers there are around and take comfort from them. And be prepared to use all the professional services available. It is no admission of defeat to need doctors, child guidance clinics, teachers, psychiatrists, educational psychologists. You are doing a hard task, your youngster has had a rough ride if he hasn't found a family before teenage, and at some point, any or all of you may need help. Find it and take it – you have a right to it. Often help is more readily available than people realize. For instance, you can walk into a child guidance clinic and ask: you don't need to be referred by anyone else. Try to obtain your local authority's guide or handbook to all the services available in your area. You may be surprised how many there are.

Finance
Teenagers are expensive. Their clothes cost a lot, and many of them are very fashion-conscious. They need pocket money; the activities most of them enjoy are expensive, and they feel humiliated if they haven't got the right gear for the right occasion. They may eat a lot; they may smoke or drink. They

may bring home friends (and it's important that they can) who will also eat and drink anything you provide – and more. If you are fostering, even as a prelude to a possible adoption, inquire about enhanced allowances. Most local authorities are generous in this respect, in my experience. Ask them about initial equipment – bedding, etc. and clothes: no child should arrive with only the clothes he is wearing. He can be kitted out before he comes, or better still, you can ask for a grant to buy new clothes for the youngster, which is usually favourably considered. New school uniform may be an item the local authority can cover, and certainly it is a major one.

A teenager is two people: a child and an adult. If you can work out which he is at any given moment, you have a head start. Good luck!

1979

CHAPTER 6

Changing places: introducing another child into an existing family

Readers of the PPIAS Newsletter will probably be familiar with descriptions of children which end, 'He needs an adoptive family where he will be the youngest or only child.' This may be the social worker's idea of an ideal family for an emotionally deprived older child, but it could happen that when inquiries about the child begin to be made and the 'right' family emerges it doesn't exactly fit this decription. The child who is to be placed will need the freedom to regress, to behave as the youngest; but the existing children of the family may all be younger than he is or he may be sandwiched somewhere in the middle! When everyone has to change places in this way there will inevitably be repercussions. If the new child becomes the eldest in the family, the former King of the Castle in the family hierarchy may resent being dethroned, especially when he has to tolerate behaviour from the newcomer that is more usually associated with a much younger child. If the placement is made in the middle of a family, the older children may grumble about having another 'baby' around, someone who interferes with their games. The younger children, on the other hand, whilst they have gained a rival for their parents' attention, may benefit from the fact that their new sibling, though older than they are, sometimes plays and behaves in the way they do.

The birth of a baby in a 'normal' family changes the relationship between an existing child and his parents. The arrival of an older child will have a much more dramatic impact on the dynamics of the family. The accounts which follow illustrate that 'changing places' in this way can work, despite problems, if all the members of the family are able to discuss what is happening and openly explore their feelings for one another.

Adoption: the inside story

- Michael, our natural son, was nine and Jimmy, our adopted child, just ten months, when we decided to adopt a three-and-a-half-year-old, Billy, who was of mixed race and had spent all his years in the same foster home.

  Bringing Billy home was an experience. For the first few days he was either curled up with a blanket, moaning, or following Bob around, never letting him out of his sight. He called us 'the man' and 'the lady', and it was a while before he became brave enough to call us Mummy and Daddy. He was very obedient, and often displayed an artificial cheerfulness, as if he thought that this was the way we would like him best. He did not trust us. He had been badly hurt by his other parents, and he was protecting himself the best way he could. He was very afraid to speak up for what he wanted, and he would often break into tears because we had not anticipated what he had not the courage to ask for.

  At first Bob and I felt a bit uncomfortable with Billy. We felt a tremendous compassion for this small child, but we did not feel the affection that we had felt for Jimmy when we had brought him home at two and a half months. Billy was like a stranger in our family. He had had experiences which we had not shared and which he could not relate to us. Being a real family meant living together and sharing experiences, and we needed time to build our own set of experiences; and only with that did we begin to develop a deep affection for him. As Billy became more familiar with his surroundings and his new family, his whole mood changed, and he emerged from this traumatic move as a cheerful, outgoing little boy, very eager to please. He gradually began to ask for things he wanted, but many times suffered in silence. Only now is a wall of uncertainly beginning to crumble, for it takes a while to iron out all the difficulties of living together.

  Bringing up a middle child did not upset the balance of our family at all. If anything it has enhanced it. Jimmy and Billy are very close; they have the usual brotherly squabbles, but there is an underlying bond that is very strong. We can partly account for it by the fact that Billy knows that Jimmy came to us under similar circumstances. Rather than one child who is different we have two who are alike. Michael has adjusted very well to having two brothers within a year; his biggest concern is keeping four grubby hands out of his belongings!

  1973

- We added an older child into the middle of the family. Our experiences have, I feel, illustrated how important it is that parents should be aware of the different rates at which relationships are formed by each child in the family. It may require a great deal of understanding and perhaps tolerance; how easily an adoption could be jeopardized by a sibling whose problems were not being fully appreciated. I think most children respond with enthusiasm when discussing the idea of adding a new child to the family, but until the new brother or sister stops being a source of fantasy and becomes a reality, they can't possibly realize just what it may mean to them.

When our fourth child, Kate, joined the family, aged six, our eldest was seventeen. Like all our children, she had naturally been involved in discussions and in our decision on adopting another child. She was mature enough to realize what problems lay ahead. Our youngest, adopted as a baby and then three-and-a-half, was just delighted to have a constant companion to share her bedroom, bathtime, meals and toys. Of course there have been the usual jealousies, squabbles and whacks, but there are also hours spent in blissful play and sharing. Our son of eleven has an outgoing, generous nature and I had always felt he would have no problems in accepting another child in the family. Unfortunately, it was he who very soon showed signs of being perturbed. To our surprise, he said he felt that we didn't need to adopt her, and asked if she could just remain as a foster child. He was adamant that he did not want her to leave the family, but something was obviously bothering him. After several talks with him we were certain that it had nothing to do with her mixed-race background, nor the fact that he had been hoping to have a brother rather than yet another sister. It eventually became clear that he had very definite feelings as to what 'sister' meant to him in the way of relationship and love. (He had a deep, close and secure love for his sister six years older than himself, and he adored his baby sister.) Therefore he felt guilty that he did not have the same sort of feelings for this new, shy, little stranger whom he was now expected to accept as a sister.

I hastened to assure him that I did not love her in the same way as I loved the three children I had known and cared for since babyhood. None of us had had enough time to allow love to grow to the same depth. I told him that I was sure that there would be great thrills ahead for us all as we discovered week by week just how much that love was growing, and how much she meant to us all. He seemed visibly to sigh with relief as guilt was lifted from him, and it was amazing to watch how, from that time, their relationship developed as they grew closer, discovering how much fun they could have together in spite of their age difference.

I feel that he became the first in our family to have a truly natural and easy relationship with Kate, helping, teasing, and encouraging her just as any brother would normally react with a younger sister. He is extremely proud of her smallest achievements, misses her when she is not at home, and is upset when she occasionally suffers pain or distress. Perhaps we had not expected him, on finding himself faced with a new intimate situation, to question his own depth of feelings for us all. Perhaps also he began to wonder about our love for him if we could overnight accept, and love in the same way, this new sister.

1975

- We finally met our eldest daughter, Lisa, in July 1979 when she was just 11. She had only been in care for nine months, following the death of her mother and the breakdown of her placement with the guardians of her mother's choice. Our whole family, Michael, aged seven, Timothy, aged three and a half and Joanna, aged 18 months, met her on a memorably sunny day when we went strawberry picking. Lisa came to stay with us for two weekends, then five days, and finally came to live with us only four weeks after our first meeting.

She made a very close bond with Joanna, and the boys welcomed her as a friend. Lisa desperately wanted a family and so tried very hard to fit in. She exhibited a number of problems such as enuresis, food fads and a tendency towards hypochondria. She could not remember having been dry for more than four nights in a row, and she arrived with a good supply of linen provided by her helpful local authority. After a few weeks the periods of her being dry increased and eventually we felt that, with the right suggestions (although she is a very heavy sleeper), she might be encouraged to be dry permanently. So, contrary to all the concepts concerning enuresis, we told Lisa, when she was wet one morning, that we felt she could do better and that she did not need to be wet – and it has worked! She has had no accidents for nearly eight months, and says that she cannot remember now what it was like to be wet. Her food fads were a minor irritation at first, and to play safe she would say she did not like something without even trying it. However, she gradually tried everything, and she and Michael are now known as 'the gannets'. Lisa's tendency towards hypochondria was terribly annoying. Whatever any of the children suffered from, she did as well, and not a day went by without her suffering from aching legs, arms, eyes etc. Sympathy ran thin at times, but she is greatly improved now, only having 'mystery' illnesses when there are upheavals in our routine, i.e. visitors or unusual happenings at school.

We adopted Lisa a year to the day after she came to live with us. She enjoys a typical big sister/mothering relationship with Joanna and occasionally with Timothy; she and Michael swap insults, but he still likes to kiss her goodnight! The hardest relationship to form was that with her Dad; she had been brought up in an almost totally female world, but after a year they enjoy a close relationship, forged in part by their love of swimming (at which the rest of us remain outclassed). For Michael the advent of an elder sister has enabled him to grow in confidence as well as stature, and for Lisa the age gap between them has enabled her to speak with authority and gain a greatly improved self-image. When she came to us she lacked confidence and would not try anything new. Now, with her growing maturity, she is finding her place in the wider community.

Lisa has filled a gap in our family of which we were unaware until her arrival, and we could not now envisage life without her. I suppose the most revealing point about the last year is our own feelings and our ability to speak about them to each other. At times, for very small things, we felt positively evil and rejecting towards her and were upset by these awful thoughts. One incident stands out very clearly. Lisa had been away for the weekend to stay with a school friend. On her return she hardly greeted us, was sullen, withdrawn and almost rude – she did not seem to want us or any contact with us at all. Now this seems very minor and paltry, but at the time we felt very hurt and rejected, and so in return we had rejecting thoughts about her and actually said so to each other. To find that we both felt the same helped to make us feel less guilty about these unspeakable thoughts! When I spoke to Lisa about her visit away she said she felt most strange coming home again for the first time – thus explaining her out-of-character behaviour. At times even now I am annoyed and hurt by her behaviour; however, we are now able to talk things through with her and all feel much better for it!

1980

- We have two mixed-race daughters, adopted as babies, now aged five and three and a half. This year we decided to enlarge our family and adopt a seven-year-old boy. We were quite happy that the older girl, Kay, would accept an older child. She preferred an older brother to a baby one, and we also told her that although she wouldn't be the eldest child any more, she would always be the eldest girl in the family. We were aware that she could be overlooked, as she is quite quiet – and we would have to make sure she wasn't. Our social worker said (and we agreed with her) that the younger girl, Celia, had a far more dominant character, and if she had been the elder they wouldn't have considered placing an older child next to her.

We met Mark in May and he moved in at the end of June. The one thing that worried us most about having an older child was whether the children would all get on, and what we would do if they didn't. Not long after Mark moved in, Kay started hitting her friends (quite out of character) and hitting Mark for no reason, as though she wanted us to come and tell her off – it seemed to be a cry for attention. In the house she was withdrawn, miserable, very low, and wouldn't talk at meal-times; when asked questions, the others would answer for her, which we had to stop. I should say Mark and Celia are similar in character. Anyway, we had a talk with Kay and told her we still loved her just as much as before, and, that we had enough love for all the children; that Mark was part of our family now, and that we needed her help to make him welcome. Since then she has been fine – really happy and more confident in herself.

Although Kay is a lot happier with Mark, he still seems a bit jealous of her. He always has to be better than her at everything, which doesn't bother her in the least. He is a lot more protective towards her and gets on better with Celia. We wonder if a lot of it is connected with his feelings about his mentally handicapped six-year-old sister, and whether she has had more attention than he in the past, or whether he feels guilty about liking Kay when he already has a sister about that age, and can accept Celia more easily as she is so much younger. Kay is similar in character to his sister. His coming has had an effect on the girls, apart from teaching them rude rhymes and words – we quickly stopped him from saying them, but they have passed them on to their friends, which isn't going down too well with other mothers in our street!

We feel so far we have had an easy time. He has done all the things you are warned about – lie, steal, cheat, be abusive – but they were all shortlived. We were firm with him. If he cheated, we stopped the game instantly – and he loves playing games. If he starts again, we will know something is really upsetting him. Mark is a boy who, when he wants something, will give his all, and he is doing that now to be part of our family. He is very lovable and affectionate, a good comic and mimic, and likes to have a go at everything. He loves 'fights' with his new Dad, which we feel also gets rid of a lot of his tension and has introduced physical contact with a man, which is something he hadn't known before. He is thrilled to have Grandad, who spoils him terribly, just as he does the girls, and to have uncles and aunts. Some of the time he acts like the teenagers who have been his main companions for four years, sometimes like a two-year-old, but more and more he is just an ordinary, outgoing, mischievous, full-of-fun, seven-year-old boy.

1980

- Having two natural children of our own, aged five and one, we decided to adopt an older child. At first we found some opposition, due to the fact that the adopted child would be the eldest in the family, rather than the youngest; we began to think we should never find the right child. One agency, contacted through the Newsletter, wanted us to farm our children out for eight hours, whilst we were interviewed on our own some way from home! We finally met John through our own social services adoptions unit. He was an 11-year-old orphan, whose father had recently died. We had the usual run-up of visits, weekend stays, etc., with the normal problems of age regression, acting out and sulking, and found the whole experience extremely demanding – at times testing the bonds within the family to the utmost. The one type of problem we expected – jealousy from our 'own' children – just did not occur. Despite John's unwillingness to share anything, our five-year-old son just worshipped him from the moment he arrived, followed him everywhere, refused to let him sulk and defended him if we criticized him at all! John could regress to an earlier age by playing with the younger children without feeling guilty about doing so. Our daughter, at one year old, just thought another adult had joined the family, and of course can not now remember a time when John was not with us. Writing this two years on, I can only say it has worked out very well for us. We just have the normal trials and troubles that having three lively children brings. I'm writing this because I feel that restricting adopted children to being the youngest in a family may deprive them of a happy home which could work out well for them. It certainly has worked well for us!

1984

CHAPTER 7

A ready-made family

For some childless couples whose chances of adopting a baby are very slim, a sibling group may be the best and certainly the quickest way to build a family. At least they will have only one lot of interviews and one set of medical examinations! But, just as the unexpected birth of twins into a family can come as a shock — twice the work as well as twice the joy — imagine what it must be like for a couple who have been married several years and who are used to doing whatever they want, more or less whenever they want to, suddenly to have placed with them a ready-made family of not just one, but two, three and sometimes more children; not babies who sleep for most of the day either, but the bigger, noisier variety of children! All that extra work and probably no time left to do the things they used to do, at least in the beginning!

Earlier chapters have outlined some of the emotional difficulties which an older child can bring to his new family. Multiply these by two or three and life might seem to be in danger of becoming extremely complicated indeed. Add a dash of built-in sibling rivalry and the mixture could become explosive. Whilst there is no set recipe for survival — each family has its own strategems for winning through — the following ingredients seem essential: a strong healthy body, an indomitable sense of humour, perseverance, common sense, mountains of patience, as well as the proverbial eyes in the back of your head! And, however tough the going, there does seem to be a consensus amongst the families that their lives are richer and fuller and that, like the unexpected twins in a 'normal' family, the ready-made adopted family brings its joys along with the hard work.

A ready-made family

- 'Aren't you real saints!' 'Oh, you are marvellous! I really think you're so good taking on four girls like that. How on earth do you cope?' People tell their children about us, saying that it's just like a fairy story, how these four orphan sisters were rescued from a children's home and have come to live in a cottage in the country with horses, dogs, cats, etc. Nobody believes us when we try to talk honestly about how and why we wanted to do it, so usually we just sidestep the issue. Now we'll try to tell the truth. First, we were very lucky. We all met at an adoption party. We went looking for a boy and a girl aged six or seven, and we met four girls aged nine to 13. It was love at first sight. We happily glossed over the obvious problems such as finance and accommodation. Lots of people told us we were taking on too much, but like young lovers we persisted. Eventually, the children arrived.

We waited anxiously for the emotional problems to occur, having had so many warnings of what to expect. They did arise, and were often quite earth-shattering. We all have fairly violent tempers, and four furious girls plotting revolutions and revenge upstairs was not uncommon, while Mum and Dad opened the sherry downstairs and tried to recover. But most problems were settled by a mixture of intelligence, grim determination and perseverance, of which we all needed a lot. Material problems were also solved remarkably rapidly. Two bedrooms turned into four cubbyholes with the aid of a few sheets of hardboard. Friends were informed that we really needed any old clothes they did not want. All, including Mum, are better dressed now than ever before, without buying any new clothes at all! Extra-large saucepans, frying pans, plates, beds, sheets, blankets had to be bought, as did a tumble drier, but we were paid back for these by the borough. Our holidays away must now be camping; last summer was glorious – the weather was grey, but that was about all that went wrong. Eight people (including two stepchildren) plus two dogs in an estate car and trailer must be seen to be believed. We wonder the car stood the strain. The looks we get when we go out – 'How can anyone have six children so similar in age?' All of them say with pride, 'I've got one brother and four sisters,' etc. They get very cross if we tell anyone the details of how we got such a large family.

Both of us have full-time teaching jobs, so that the everyday life we lead must be organized, but only inasmuch as everyone does their share. One person feeds the horses every morning at seven, then walks the dogs. Someone else does it at night, and our non-horserider feeds the rest of the animals. House cleaning is done once a week, unless special visitors come, and this is done by all. Washing is done by Mum, and collected and ironed by each person (15 loads a week) Shopping is planned and done monthly. We live off the freezer and the vegetable patch. Homework is religiously stuck to, amounting to perhaps one and a half to two hours a night. They all had a lot to catch up on at school. Now we all enjoy it, and it seems to go on longer, whereas at first we had tantrums. We have dinner parties once a month for fun, and we all sit and eat special meals by candlelight and talk for anything up to two hours. Above all we have learned the need to talk, to work as a team. We were once asked, 'What if someone doesn't want to do it?' No-one ever doesn't, we don't know why. We do know we all have a lot of fun, more than we could have imagined. We work, play and talk hard, but above all we love each other. Our family have given us more life than we thought possible; the work and the trials are worth it.

1980

- Derek was describing to a friend the nice things about being adopted: you get, he said, a Mummy and Daddy and a house. But the best thing of all is having a sister. The friend had been adopted too, but as a baby, a distinct disadvantage in the eyes of our son, who came to us at the age of six and a half and promptly chose himself a sister.

We had an introductory period of six months' weekly visiting with Derek in order to prepare him for the change of environment, as he had been stable and happy in the children's home. His understanding of what was happening was remarkable. This constantly came through in the way he pulled together his new experiences, although he rarely referred directly to adoption. On the day he came 'for good' however, he did so – and asked us to adopt his 'sister', a little girl of whom he had been particuarly fond in the home.

We had been advised by his social worker that Derek would need our undivided attention and care over a long period before he would be able to settle fully, and that we should not contemplate introducing a second child into the family for at least two years; it was essential for him to be an only child in order to appreciate and accept new family relationships, love, responsibilities. Two weeks after he came, however, we made tentative enquiries of the house mother, and learned that the little girl in question was available for adoption. We decided that Derek's idea was a good one and neither an expression of his own insecurity nor a testing of us; we talked about it with him, telling him that a three-year-old sister would not be all fun, that she would take up a lot of our time and doubtless try the patience of all of us! We also discussed with him the positive aspects of fuller family life. This was delicate but essential – we had to be reasonably sure, *before* taking our proposal to the soical services, that we really wanted this second child, that Derek would be able to cope emotionally, and that the advantages were sufficiently strong to overcome the normal pattern of placements of older children by the social services. And yet, if our request had been rejected, it would almost certainly have damaged Derek's relationship with us.

Fortunately, discussions with the social worker led her to agree that her previous understanding of his needs was – already – no longer valid and that we were in a better position to make such a judgement than she was. Derek had needed a family; he had been acutely aware of his lack of parents, but more than that, his perception of family life required extension – to grandparents (when he met his new grandmother, he quite definitely had a far stronger feeling of belonging to a family than he had had before) – and to brothers and sisters. So we began with a sister! We were lucky, since at this stage the introduction of an unknown child would have been difficult, but the two children knew each other, and were already attached to each other; they had shared experiences, one of which was their mixed racial background which was an important factor in deciding for all of us. We were lucky, too, in that the social workers (and Monique was in the care of a different agency) accepted our analysis of the situation, and Monique was placed with us only six months after Derek.

Derek was delighted; he informed all his school friends that he was to have a sister, which caused some bewilderment because none of them had ever been able to predict the sex of babies arriving in their families! When she came, the fuss made of Monique by Derek's friends was extraordinary. The fuss Derek and Monique made of each other was extraordinary too. They would accost anyone and everyone in the street, in shops, and announce with great pride, 'Derek is my brother', 'Monique is my sister.' 'We're going to be adopted.' Just before Monique arrived, Derek, who previously had called us by our first names, declared his intention of calling us Mummy and Daddy because it would help his sister to understand. And he did, from then on. He explained to her what adoption and families were about; we would hear him telling her how he too had found it strange at first and had got used to it! He would tell us about her past, the mutual background of the children's home.

His delight, first in having been chosen by us, and having himself chosen us, and then in having chosen his sister, has been constant. All this choosing leads to complications: they are both threatening to run away if we don't adopt the little boy next door! The placing of the two children, both labelled as 'hard to place' and as needing to be the only child for a considerable length of time, has been a total success: both have an increased awareness of what family life is and enjoyment of it. They share the same adoption day, which took some managing, but which somehow completed their sense of belonging to each other and to us. They are now working on us to find a further brother or sister.

1975

- We had no kids and led a quiet, peaceful life which sometimes became boring. Suddenly two boys and a girl aged six, seven and eight descended on us. Sunday used to be a time to enjoy the crossword and finish it by cheating if necessary. Now we dash it off, usually without completing it. We used to watch TV – now we spend the time on the kids' three Rs. Instead of departing to bed when we feel like it, we have late-night talks about their problems. We don't allow them to sleep in our five-feet-wide bed: two's cosy, five's a crowd.

  What to feed them on? They eat more than I do. Cook a special meal and they aren't hungry; a quick rushed snack and they are starving. Instead of beetroot on the table, it lands on the floor. Raise your voice and a young one says, 'Are you getting cross?' What used to be a nice quiet breakfast for two is now a mad dash for five. Jobs taking two days before, now, with extra willing hands, take a week. Make pastry and there is more flour on the floor than on the table. Make a cake and it is necessary to remember not to put the utensils straight into the sink, as they have to be shared out between three for licking purposes. Still, our number two son is very appreciative of home-made cakes; make a large quantity of baking and it doesn't see the freezer.

  You can't be ill because there isn't time. We have become involved in a different social life as, being parents, we get involved in their activities. One Saturday last summer we could have attended three functions at once!

1977

A ready-made family

● Here we were at last, sitting with a social worker who was telling us about a little boy called Philip whom she was trying to place in a permanent foster home, and ours could possibly be that home. It had been decided that Philip, a child with many problems, would need a home where there were no other children, and we fitted that category. The social worker went on to explain:

'He is one of a pair of twins, who, since being taken into care at the age of two, have to be kept separated most of the time because together they are uncontrollable. They are West Indian, six years old, educationally subnormal, destructive, overactive and have to be restrained often because of their aggression. They suffer from a mild form of epilepsy which causes one twin to have an occasional, uncontrollable jerk in his left arm, the other twin in his right . . . . one is left-handed, the other right-handed. One boy walks on his heels, the other on his toes; they do not speak very clearly, are almost impossible to control even when not together, and often have violent temper tantrums. They have had numerous changes of children's homes because of their intolerable behaviour, and one home had five members of staff leave because they found the twins so insufferable. One even went so far as to describe Philip as being 'a sinister child'. They have been declared 'impossible to home', but we know of no child who needs love and a secure home more than Philip, who is believed to be the more deeply disturbed of the twins. It's asking a lot, but if you are interested we will arrange a meeting at the children's home where he is now.'

We have since been asked why we did not rush out of the door there and then; but we had been through a great deal because we so wanted a child, and my husband and I both knew what the other was thinking and nodded our agreement, so the arrangements were made for us to meet Philip that very afternoon. As we drove to the children's home we felt very nervous. 'This is it at last,' we thought, 'a chance for us, and a chance for this disturbed little boy.'

The warden of the home suggested to Philip that he might like to sit with me, and as he sat on my lap looking up at me with big, dark eyes and as he stroked my long hair, I knew that I wanted to help this child as much as I could. It was not love at first sight but a realization of Philip's needs which drew us to him. We knew that it would take a very long time before he could come to love us – in fact there was a very strong possibility that we would never receive any affection from him – and because of that we felt, even more than any pity or compassion, a great feeling of determination to make it all work. This little stranger aroused such an assortment of emotions in me all at once, that I don't think I could list them all.

From then on, each time we saw Philip we felt more and more of a commitment to him. In fact I believe we were committed totally right from the start. We had worried about the welfare of Sam, the other twin, from the time we first learned about the twins, and it was not long before we admitted that we would like to share our attachment to Philip with Sam as well. We asked our social worker if there was any chance of us taking on Sam; she and her senior were firmly against this, mostly for our sakes more than the boys, but they agreed to our meeting Sam, hoping I suspect that we might then be put off from our crazy notion. We met them on bank holiday when they were coming from their boarding school (for educationally subnormal children who were disturbed and had other problems) and were to deliver them to their separate children's homes in London for the holiday weekend. When we saw them together we could not tell the difference. In fact I thought Sam was Philip; it was impossible to tell the difference except for their clothes. When we took them to the homes, we found there had been some mix-up and they were both to stay in the same one. We had planned to fetch Philip each day over the weekend, take him to our home and really try to get to know him, and in the circumstances we certainly could not bring ourselves to take just Philip and leave poor Sam behind in the home. We could not get in touch with our social worker because it was the weekend so we took it on ourselves to include Sam and in doing so found, as we suspected, that we felt the same way about Sam as we had about Philip.

The days were hard, starting with an hour's journey to collect the boys, then an hour home with them. The days at home were hectic, with us having to be with Sam and Philip for every second; we could not let them out of our sight for a moment. They were unbelievably quick to find things they shouldn't find and do things they shouldn't do, then after each tiring day we would have the hour's journey back to the home, then another hour back to our own home. We could see the problems ahead, but felt we had to have both the twins – after all, the only stable thing each one had had in his life was the other twin, even if they did spend much of their time together being aggressive towards each other.

After the weekend the battle began to persuade the social workers to let us have them both, and they were very reluctant. We must have nearly driven them mad with our pestering but eventually the unenthusiastic words came: 'If you're mad enough you can try it.' We were overjoyed, and arrangements were made for us to have them over one night to see how we managed. In the morning they got up and hit the house like a whirlwind! In less than two minutes they had switched off the boiler, put metal things in the washing machine, knocked the dog's water bowl over, sent all the cat's food and milk down the back of the freezer, and switched off the electricity supply – that was honestly in only two minutes when they raced downstairs before we did. Oh, yes – we could see what we were in for! Even the dogs became exhausted by trying to keep up with the action and eventually retired upstairs to collapse and sleep it off. The twins were to stay at their special boarding school for a further year, and during this time we had them at home with us at every possible time and we suffered nightmares we had never dreamed of. There was wanton destruction, mischief in the extreme, violence towards each other, violence towards us – me particularly – language which I hardly knew existed, throwing things, threats, deliberate disobedience and resentment every time we had to discipline them. We had to try to keep law and order but it was incredibly difficult.

We had received a great deal of advice from our social worker, the child psychologist who had always dealt with the twins, and also from the headmistress of their school, who was extremely helpful and backed us up all the way. We had been strongly advised to try and ignore as much of this terrible behaviour as possible, but when a child has his teeth firmly sunk into your side, it is very hard to ignore it! However, we made as little of it as possible, and called their bluff on many threats. If one of them said, 'I'll throw a brick through the window', we would shrug, unimpressed, and walking away would reply, 'OK, we could do with a new window anyway', and because they wanted to do what we did not want them to do they would usually go on to something else. We could not guarantee that this would always work, but if I had shouted 'No! Don't break the window' I can guarantee they would have done so. I became an intent watcher of wrestling on television, and various holds for restraining certainly came in useful, and for weeks I was covered in bruises from my efforts, but gradually the frightening, aggressive tantrums decreased, so did my bruises, and we felt we were getting somewhere at last. We had known that we must be behind them supporting them for better or worse ... the tantrums which could last for four hours were certainly the 'worse', and so after several months we were able to look towards the future 'better'. Their trust in us was growing stronger all the time, and as they became more and more settled with us I believe they could actually begin to believe that someone wanted them at last. The initial testing-out process was over, and the intense episodes reduced from about three a day to more like three a week.

The twins needed tremendous encouragement, not just for doing things which were extra good, but for actually not being naughty ... we praised them when they didn't use violence towards us in a tantrum, or when they did not swear or when they did not try to break things; sometimes, when a day had been particularly bad, we had to think of something to praise. It must have been very hard for these youngsters suddenly to conform to a normal family life which was far from what they had ever been used to, and being backward they were unable to understand so many things: it was a big adjustment to expect them to make, and the resulting trauma was inevitable.

It is now almost eighteen months since we first met Philip and Sam. They have left their boarding school and will soon begin to attend a local special school as day boys. Any slight worry on their part or anything they imagine could be a threat to their newfound security produces outbursts like those we saw during the first months, and the present changes have indeed brought forth more frequent trouble with both boys. Sam can be readily affectionate to us and anyone else – how genuine this affection is I cannot at this time say – but Philip has also recently been able to allow himself to show some affection. He finds this difficult but I feel it is genuine on his part, mainly because it has taken him so long to be able to demonstrate anything but frequent aggression – which still lies only just below the surface and does not need much provocation to produce again.

We have experienced feelings towards Sam and Philip of pity, annoyance, compassion, rage, despair, determination, understanding, closeness, responsibility, commitment absolute and entire whatever the future may bring, and, most of all, satisfaction, happiness and love.

1977

CHAPTER 8

Bonding: letting the love grow

The preparatory work for 'bonding' between a mother and child normally begins, on the mother's part, during the nine months before birth. Likewise, adoptive parents can conjure up ideas about the child they are waiting to have placed with them and make themselves 'ready' for his arrival. After birth, or placement, as the parents respond to the child's needs the bonding process is developed and strengthened.

It is a slow process. It does not happen the moment a baby is born. Natural parents and their children weave their bonds of affection over the months and years of their lives together. Adoptive parents, especially those adopting older children, should not expect instant results either. Youngsters who have been uprooted from their natural parents at an early age and who have not experienced the usual interaction between mother and child will find developing new bonds with others extremely difficult. Adoptive parents attempting to graft these children into their families speak of the frustration experienced in giving attention and affection but receiving little in return. Existing members of the family may have strong feelings of family loyalty — of sticking together — which may be totally alien to the newcomer. For him to develop family bonds he must be given time: time to relax and build his relationship with them based on a new set of mutual experiences; time to let the love grow.

The families whose stories appear in this chapter describe how they attempted to tie the bonds of affection with their adopted children, albeit painfully and slowly, and sadly in one case, with the feeling that the bond that was being tied was one of commitment rather than love.

Adoption: the inside story

- We first met Elizabeth when she was seven, with her social worker, in the park, at the beginning of April. She had been in residential care all her life, except for two unsuccessful fostering attempts. One of two other couples who visited the home were told quite plainly by her that if they thought she was going home with them to be 'their' little girl they had better 'go away' because she *wasn't*. After three very successful visits to us, one overnight, she came at the end of that same month to stay for good. Because of the previous failures and her particular character, everyone felt it best if she were moved very quickly, once she (and we) thought this a good idea!

From then on till Christmas we thought we were slowly progressing. We had problems, of course. There were attention-seeking, show-off scenes, noisy verbal aggressiveness, and highly emotional bedtime scenes. These were deliberately provoked, usually by a very small naughty incident which was then blown up out of proportion by her to make sure we would give her lots of verbal and physical reassurance, and proof of our love. This was repeated nightly for many weeks, lasting anything from 20 to 45 minutes, but as it became less intense we felt we could become a little firmer and not always allow it to happen, and slowly it disappeared.

Her efforts to divide the family, however, were more worrying. She had survived seven years of residential care reasonably unharmed because she was a tough, fighting extrovert. Somehow she had to come out on top, and of course this had to be at someone else's expense. She tried to continue this with us, but found that in a close, loving family, although everyone was ready to give her all kinds of support and love, no-one would tolerate being divided from each other. Although she had such tremendous spirit and such a sense of humour and fun, she did not want to please any of us, least of all my husband. At the time when the adoption date was set things looked pretty precarious, but we thought that once it was all over and she really belonged to the family she would gain the confidence she presently lacked.

As soon as she discovered that a date was fixed she really threw the book at us. The bedtime scenes returned, she tried to shock my husband in particular with the dirtiest lavatorial words she had learned, used in lurid descriptions invariably at meal times. She would beg him to put her to bed, and as he bent down to kiss her she would violently pull his hair or nearly choke him by pulling on his tie. The final row came one night when she shouted at him, 'and anyway, it's up to me to decide if I want to stay here, not you.' This was something we had not bargained for. By this time we were so distraught and emotionally drained that we felt cornered and totally unprepared to take on the responsibility of the adoption which was imminent. We felt we all needed a breathing space, and so asked for a postponement of the hearing. We were lucky to have a marvellous social worker and talked to her at great length. In particular we found her most illuminating on behaviour patterns of deprived children. After some days of objective thinking, we realized that we had become too involved in the child's external and superficial behaviour to view things in their true perspective. We discovered that, in the irritations and hurtings in the petty things of everyday life, we had lost sight of the original purpose of giving her the love and home she had always been denied, and that this deprivation had made her behave as she did.

We told Elizabeth it might be a long time before the judge could see us, as he was very busy. Immediately, the tension broke and our relationships became better than at any previous time. She began to talk about her natural mother, very hesitantly at first, but with greater ease each time. It became apparent that she had built up the enormous fantasy that one day her 'real mummy' would come for her. This made us all realize that all the previous attempts at introductions had failed because she feared her mother would be unable to find her if she were no longer at the children's home. This also explained her reluctance to change her name. Once we had talked through all this and had promised her to help her find her mother if she still wanted to when she was older, she relaxed completely and spoke with pleasure and excitement about going to see the judge. For our part, with all the tension gone, we decided to apply for a new hearing date and she was adopted about six weeks later.

It is now three months since the adoption. Life goes on, some days good, some days bad, but they are never boring! We realize that however much you think you know in theory, it's never the same when it actually happens.

1975

- We have two children born to us and one adopted as a baby; and I think we rather took it for granted that we would be able to add a school-age child to our family. Alicia came to us aged six, very much in need of new parents, and quickly put roots down, doing all she could to please us. She really was a child with no apparent problems, other than shyness. We did realize that it would take time to get to know a six-year-old and begin to build up a meaningful relationship, but I don't think we were prepared for the time this would take, nor for the feelings she would arouse in us. I can look back now on days of overwhelming guilt when I realized that I did not love her as I did the other children. I was ashamed at constantly being irritated by her when all she wanted was my attention. I can remember wishing that she had come to us with problems, tantrums, bedwetting, nightmares, anything that would give me scope to help her and, through therapeutic parenting, perhaps begin to build a close relationship. Instead I had an obedient child who would do anything I asked of her without question, and whose conversation was never more than trivial questions about time or meals – I was therefore forcibly aware of my lack of feelings. I tried physical contact but, being unused to cuddling, she did not know how to respond and, although pleased to sit on my knee, she would quickly feel awkward and stiff. Unfortunately, having had no experience of men in her life, she was afraid and uncertain of my husband, and in the early days avoided any contact with him. He wisely paid little attention to her, allowing her plenty of time to get used to the familiarity with which he treated the other children, and then slowly and casually including her in conversations and games.

I think that several things happening at much the same time helped me to realize that our relationship was growing daily, if at an imperceptibly slow rate. Friends, teachers and neighbours commenting on her progress, and on how obviously happy and integrated she had become, gave me confidence. Hearing of several other adoptive parents going through somewhat similar emotional worries helped me to shed my guilt feelings. I realized that it was perfectly possible to be a reasonably good parent and love one's children in different ways. Perhaps most significant of all, when we went on holiday without the children I realized for the first time just how much I missed her, and found myself lying in bed at night worrying in case she was not well or happy at home – she really had become my daughter. Now, nearly five years later and with one more child in the family, we are aware that relationships do not happen overnight, are not always dramatically established, and can have painful moments. What is needed is patience, understanding and commitment, and the love will grow.

1978

Bonding: letting the love grow

- We first met Joe five years ago, when he was five years old. We visited him at the children's home where he had lived for one and a half years. We were introduced to all the children as visitors. Most of them made a fuss of us, clambering on our knees and demanding attention, but Joe totally ignored us. Next time we went he had seen our scrapbook, and readily came to the park with us and our other children, who were then aged ten, eight and three years. The youngest, a girl, had been adopted as a baby. The two older boys were very impressed by Joe, as he did such daring and dangerous tricks on the swings. He called us Mum and Dad immediately, which felt very strange to us.

After three months of coming home for days, then weekends, Joe came home for good. This was at the beginning of the summer holidays. By the end of six weeks I was never so pleased to see anyone off to school. He wasn't really any trouble, he was just there all the time. He did everything he was told to without question. His little sister became especially bossy, but he showed her a lot of affection, hugging her when she was upset. He also got on well with the boys, continually wrestling with them. With us it was different; whenever either of us tried to get close to him we felt shut out by his completely blank expression. He never really seemed pleased to see us and when I went to his school to help, which I did regularly, he completely ignored me. I began to question myself, and felt there must be something quite wrong with me because at times I disliked him so much. At these times I remember hating myself. I remember, too, talking to someone about a problem I had with Joe and she said, 'Things will improve as he begins to feel secure with you and knows that you love him.' I felt so guilty afterwards. I should have said, 'But I don't love him' – but I didn't have the courage.

We were very determined that things would get better and that he would become a real member of the family. We adopted him when he was seven years old. Slowly he became part of us. We didn't notice him all the time. Although he retained his own personality, he became more like the other children. He expressed himself more, cried loudly when scolded instead of just staring at us. He looked pleased to see relations. He actually said 'hello' to me one day in the school playground. I was so pleased.

It is two years now since the last really bad patch, when, in the middle of talking to his headmaster, I burst into tears because I felt all communication had broken down between us and I felt very scared. Looking back, writing this, and realizing that I haven't felt such self-doubt for a whole two years, makes us aware that Joe is now an equal part of our family. We feel that when problems do crop up we should be able to cope with them because he is truly our child, the same as the other children. There were many times when I never thought that this would happen.

1982

- We had Daniel at just under six months and it should have been easy – as it had been with Jenny, who arrived at four months and was now rising two years. The introductory meeting seemed fraught with tension, but we both felt that once we were at home, on our own, things would be different. Not until four years later could we honestly say we had made it! Daniel had become one of us, he loved us, needed us and felt able to show his feelings openly; but it had been a long hard struggle. In between we had to deal with a baby/toddler/small boy who could not accept cuddles, could not let himself be loved and, apparently, would not love us. We carried him everywhere in an 'Easy Rider' sling until he was 12 months old, to give him the security we felt he needed, but often as not he would still scream, arch his back and struggle: trying to escape!

  Once he was mobile (at 12 months) Dan was better able to control his environment, and he learned to remove himself to his bedroom, shut the door and withdraw until he was ready to cope again. Any attempt to intervene or soothe the hurts produced more violent reactions; we had to accept that what seemed so natural to us, to hug, stroke and cuddle, was totally alien to Daniel. Discipline, too, had to change. Our relaxed approach using distraction and diversion was clearly unworkable. It seemed that Daniel needed a much firmer line, including physical punishment (which we were loth to use) and much raising of the voice. Only in this way could Dan maintain his equilibrium (although it severely disturbed ours) and survive. At three the question of playgroup arose. Dan was unready to cope with other people on his own, but we were lucky enough to become involved with an opportunity group (two-thirds handicapped children) where parents were encouraged to attend; Daniel would be one of the 'normal' children. No prizes for guessing who wouldn't sit and listen at storytime, who screamed through singing sessions and ran everyone over on the milk lorry during free play! But he was accepted, and gradually his behaviour improved – particularly if I was not around

Bonding: letting the love grow

(another hard fact to accept). One year later he entered morning school '100 per cent together', a popular, happy child who was obedient, kind and a definite 'loony'!

We can give no reasons for Daniel's disruptive behaviour, but we can say with certainty that the evening he woke up frightened, crept into the sitting room and snuggled onto my knee was the evening we knew the struggle was ending! From then on we have seen smiles, cuddles and love grow, and we are certain that Daniel will never have such big problems to face again in his life. He has worked it out!

1982

- Our son Peter, now 13 years old, arrived in our family when he was nearly seven, with a history of rejection and lack of care. I remember being very hurt initially, as the slightest physical contact with me would cause him to shrug me off, although he was prepared to accept affection from my husband. He regularly had nightmares, and tantrums were his answer to any sort of discipline we administered. His moods were unpredictable and, of course, there were sheets constantly on the line! Within a month or two things began to change. He made a friend at school and began to look less frightened. But best of all, he showed real signs of wanting to belong to us. He asked if he could call us Mummy and Daddy, and a delightful stage came when he first whispered, 'I love you.' Such were the initial stages of our 'bonding process'. About six months after Peter arrived, we had to move house, and although we feared this might prove very unsettling, in fact it brought us all much closer together. Even so, there were times when Peter found it very difficult to accept us as his family, and was very confused and uncertain about his relationships with us. Sometimes we were very uncertain about our relationship with him! It is very hard to go on loving a child when one receives little in return. However, the months and the years went by, and we had a relatively settled period of growing together.

When we adopted a baby daughter, Peter was nine years old. The security that he was accustomed to, as our only child, was threatened. He resented the attention given to her, became uncooperative, and regressed in many ways. He has now had four years to get used to her, and although the two often squabble, they are very fond of each other and the bond between them is very strong. Having a little sister (however much he may despise girls!) has made Peter identify much more with us as a family unit. Her presence in the family also makes us particularly conscious of how terribly important these early years are for healthy emotional development, and how we can never make up to Peter for all that he has missed.

Peter is now an adolescent with all the additional problems that that brings, and the emotional tugs are at times very conflicting. He is still very immature, has behavioural problems, and is probably still under-achieving at school. However, there is no doubt that we go on growing together as we share experiences, and there are many happy moments. We would find life very dull without our children. Only this morning Peter got up early to do some extra maths, then brought us a cup of tea in bed. Bless him! What would we do without him?

1982

- Clare joined our family in 1974 when she was just five, having spent most of her life in the same residential nursery. She had had no home contact for years, and the only family she knew was in her imagination. Our family consisted of Jo (father), me (mother) and Sally, who was nearly eight when Clare arrived. We had applied to the adoption resource exchange for a child of West Indian origin, not specifying age or sex, and were offered, one after another, two baby boys. They didn't feel 'right' for our family, and we did not follow up the offers. Our social worker, doubting the seriousness of our intentions, gave us the ARE's list of 'children who wait', and the description of Clare immediately attracted us. This element of choice in how she came to our family contributed to the very considerable commitment we have always had to her.

We were very happy when, after months of unpleasant wrangling with the local authority in whose care she was, Clare arrived. It was not long before I said to Jo, 'That child doesn't need a mother.' Life in an institution had equipped her with a formidable independence of spirit. She might have longed for a family intellectually, because everyone else had one, but she certainly resented any attempt at guidance or mothering. Sally's dream of a 'dear little sister', too, was quickly shattered when Clare turned out to be a bossy leader, expert at upstaging sweet-natured, dreamy little girls, even if several years older. There was the usual honeymoon period, but then things got rough. Our cosy little threesome showed no signs of developing into a similar – or any other kind of – foursome. Clare had no desire to join any of our traditional family hobbies and activities; just the fact that we liked doing something seemed to turn her off! If she was made to join us in any of the pursuits she disliked, the pleasure of them was seriously marred by her very vocal criticism. This was fair enough – we couldn't expect her to share all our tastes; more difficult to take was her rejection of all the special unwritten family rules and values, which we had never realized existed until they were challenged by a new recruit – such as supporting one another in sticky situations, putting up a united front in public. 'Why should I?' was Clare's cry when we invoked family loyalty, or consideration for another family member – like being quiet when someone was ill – as a reason for behaving in any particular way. We tried in all ways to make Clare behave like 'one of the family', including bribery, punishments and rewards, appeals to finer feelings, and just offering her consistent love in the hope that the necessary feelings would in the end arise spontaneously from within her. They didn't.

Meanwhile, Clare aggressively adopted our name and family identity to the outside world and dug herself deeply into our home and our life. It also became clear that, though her feelings for us were not filial in any conventional sense, they were nevertheless, in some other way, very strong. She hated being away from home, always wanted to know where any absent member of the family was, and, though soon having educational difficulties, was able to learn to read and write at home. Painful though we found Clare's response, year in year out, to the love we offered her, we had to admire her toughness and independence. Quite possibly, as a black girl with a white, middle-class upbringing, she would need it. Nevertheless, we clung to our dream that if we persisted long enough, we would, one day, achieve with Clare the loving and harmonious relationship for which we longed and which we thought was the only basis for a satisfactory family life.

Then Sally cracked. Clare was fiercely jealous of her, and continuous surreptitious needling over three years or so had reduced Sally from a sunny child into a nervous wreck, nail-biting, insomniac, school phobic, weepy and tempestuous by turns. Deluded by the impossible task we had set ourselves of integrating Clare into the family on the same terms as our natural child, we had failed to notice what was happening. Our new approach to the situation was not the result of a thought-out plan – it was the only way to survive. We obviously had to stop thinking of ourselves as a foursome, whose togetherness had any special meaning; we gave up canal weekends, trips to the pantomime and most other joint activities; they were anyway usually disastrous. We obviously couldn't go back to being a threesome, with one extra person on the periphery. So we just became four individuals; home and family could no longer be an end in themselves. They became a lift-off platform and refuelling station for each of us to do his own thing. For Sally this was very hard to begin with. Never a robust soul, she was packed off to relations in Germany, not speaking a word of German (and they no English) to attend a German school for a month; next she was, literally, made to go to sea (when invited on a long cruising holiday). Clare was packed off too, where possible – judo, acting club, camping, to grandmother. Perhaps it was a good thing that Jo and I became increasingly tied up with our work and with local community affairs.

So where do we stand now? Sally is 16, working hard for her O levels. Driven prematurely out of the nest, she is now very confident and mature for her age. Clare can no longer upset her. Though they have very little in common, they will at times stick up for one another and act as allies. Sally has rather grown away from us, and her life is very much outside the home. The very occasional canal weekend with her, when Clare is off somewhere, remind us that, though our threesome can never again be the same, it is possible to recapture, if only briefly, our old closeness. Clare is 13, her personality little changed from when she first came to us. She was always a survivor, but she appears to be doing better than that now, beginning to make the most of her abilities. We are very proud of her. There are still violent clashes when we try to encroach on her independence in the name of family standards, as we sometimes must. We no longer waste our breath on loving appeals, but use crude threats. Do we regret having adopted her? There are times when conflict and hostility make us feel like that momentarily. But, since we cast aside our dream of making her into a 'daughter' in a mystical sense, and gave her as much room to be herself as the survival of the rest of the family could tolerate, we have all been liberated. We have learned to get along together somehow, though our relationship is scarcely parental. It has elements of love/hate and is very committed, that is all I can say. In addition we have each of us become stronger, more tolerant and capable people, and we don't regret that.

1982

CHAPTER 9

Telling: sharing the past

'Happiness and security cannot be built on lies or fears of discovery.' Jane Rowe in her book *Yours By Choice* gives this as one of the most important reasons why adopters should tell their children that they are adopted. Concealing the truth, as some adopters did 40 or 50 years ago, often had distressing consequences: many trusting relationships were irreparably broken when the adoptees discovered that their adoptive parents had been deceiving them.

Adopted children need to know about and feel proud of their adoptive status. In simple practical terms, it may help them if they have some verbal ammunition ready to fire at those in the playground who might choose to call them names. It is very difficult to defend yourself if you don't really understand why you are being picked on in the first place. The black child adopted into a white family needs to be able to explain to school friends what might seem to them to be a rather odd family set-up. The older child adopted into a new family should feel able to talk about his past, not close the door on it as if it had never happened.

Children should be able to discuss their adoptive status — but when is the best time for parents to start 'telling', and what is the best way to approach the subject? Recent American research* has shown that pre-school age children understand very little of the real implications of being adopted. Whilst early telling is helpful in accustoming the child to the words (and gives parents valuable practice in saying them), it must be followed up by further explanations as the child's ability to grasp the concept develops. How parents tell their child will depend on the relationship they have together but, if they have begun to talk freely about the subject from very early on, they will probably find that opportunities present themselves — usually totally unexpectedly and often at inconvenient times — and the child's own curiosity will prompt discussion. If he sees that his parents are quite relaxed and comfortable about his asking questions, he will feel happy about

---

*Professor David Brodzinsky, 'New perspectives on adoption revelation', *Adoption and Fostering*, vol. 8, no. 2 (1984).

asking for more information whenever he needs it.

'Telling' need not be a painful experience. Adopters know when they are taking a child into their family that they are taking him 'whole', a complete package, which necessarily includes his past. A child adopted as a baby will want to know about his natural family although he will have no memory of them. It is the 'need to know' which adoptive parents must try to satisfy. In this respect, couples who have adopted babies have a different task from those adopting older children. The baby adopters have a 'book of blank pages' to fill in with whatever information their agency has given them; those taking on older children will sometimes have to discover what is already written on the early pages in their children's 'books' by enabling their children to recall the past, and by supplementing what the social worker can tell them with their own detective work to fill in the gaps.

The accounts that follow confirm that telling is not just done once, but all through the child's life, and that, although the child may take the initiative sometimes, adopters should also bring up the subject themselves. For most children the information provided by their adoptive parents will be sufficient to satisfy their 'need to know', but for some the telling may culminate, when they are adults, in a search for one or both of the natural parents (see Ch.11, 'Tracing'). But even this step should not cause adopters anxiety — most studies on the subject show that when adoptees do trace their natural parents, it is not because they are dissatisfied with their adoptive ones, nor do they stop thinking of the latter as their 'real' ones.

Telling: sharing the past

- They like to know (if too young at the time to remember) how you fetched them – our oldest particularly remembers an orange lollipop given to her by our son's foster mother when we went to bring him home. The girls especially like to know exactly what they were wearing, and the boys the means of transport. It is helpful to know and talk about other children or adults who were adopted. They like to know the first name of their natural parents if this is known, and where they are now – though at six years old the subject is usually dropped there, as something more interesting claims the attention.

- As far as actual words go, they are difficult to advise on, as people communicate with each other in many different ways, and what would be useful for one might be unhelpful for another. We used the word 'adopted' from a very early age – before 12 months – it helps to get used to using it oneself anyway, even if it doesn't filter through to the baby. The main thing I feel is that it is important only to say things which you yourself feel completely relaxed and happy about, otherwise your feelings will come through to the child and may distort what you are trying to say.

- There's no question of sitting down and saying, 'We've got something to tell you.' The situation is one which is lived out from day to day. The facts filter through gradually, some in answer to questions put (usually when one is negotiating a particularly difficult traffic jam or writing Happy Birthday on a cake!), some one produces spontaneously as the opportunity offers itself. The philosophy is felt by the child growing up in a warm and loving family. It's best not to have any taboos. There's plenty of repetition and interested discussion, particularly when there are siblings who develop the themes and compare notes.

- Like all children, our two adopted children love to hear incidents and episodes in their very early lives which they can no longer remember. Sticking to chronological order doesn't seem to matter in the least – 'what I did that day when I was only one year old' is just as interesting as 'the day when I first came to live here'. It is as we share the memories and factual details that the total picture builds up and becomes complete. But for each of our two there has been a stage when 'my special story' (the events leading up to and surrounding the adoption) has been in demand several times a day. It is as this 'personal history' becomes expanded as the children grow older that we've realized just how many questions to which we shall sadly never know the answers, about our children's birth, parents and families – even if we've been given very full details to tell them and even perhaps had direct contact in some way. So, as we all do have to guess, I think it's very important to remember that we should make our interpretation of this half-knowledge as positive as we can – we could well be guessing right!

- Our two 'home-grown' children were five and four years old when we acquired our Anglo-West Indian second daughter. As these were ideal ages for having stories read, I compiled a 'family story', starting from our meeting and marriage, progressing through the birth of each of the children, and leading naturally into the simplified details of the adoption and origins of their little sister. It was a very amateur effort with pin-men illustrations, but was an immediate success with the children, who demanded to hear it again and again. Now that 'little sister' is herself four years old, and she in turn loves the story, to which has been added her adopted younger brother.

1977

- Books have been written to help parents tell their children about adoption and there are quite a number of attractively illustrated books for children which many families find helpful. On the other hand, our daughter, adopted as a baby, loves to hear her 'own' story told over and over again with different details added at each telling. Long before she could talk or possibly understand the meaning of 'adoption', she knew she was our 'darling adopted daughter', whereas her elder sister was our 'darling daughter'. She was therefore always aware of a difference, but one that had no bearing on our love for both of them. Later, when she was able to ask about adoption, it was possible to begin to tell her simply and naturally that her sister grew in my tummy whereas she grew in Pauline's tummy. We have always been anxious to avoid talking of 'first Mummy' therefore implying that we were 'second Mummy and Daddy', and so have always referred to our adopted children's biological parents by their Christian names. As she is a very extrovert child I feel certain that she will always ask questions when she feels she needs more information; and as long as we continue to give her simple and truthful answers, I feel she will be satisfied.

Our other daughter, adopted as a seven-year-old, shies away from asking personal questions or referring to her life before she joined our family, and very often we feel we have to look for opportunities to refer to her first six years and to her racial background. Because this was a time when she did not have a normal family life, she is often too anxious to blot out and forget it. In an effort to help her sort out her very muddled memories, and to fill in the gaps in the information she had been previously given, we started to make a scrapbook. It took a good deal of persistence to get any relevant information from the social services department. Eventually I sent the social worker a long list of questions, saying I would be grateful if only a few of them could be answered. I knew that it was possible for him to visit her biological mother, as she had been contacted in order to sign the consent form. I included all sorts of questions in the hope of gleaning information about her early babyhood and, considering the passage of time, I was grateful for the answers I received.

We then started slowly over many months to build her scrapbook. As writing was then a considerable labour for her, I did most of the simple factual writing, leaving her to put in the important information such as the date of her birth, where she was born, her first name, etc. We were able to illustrate the book with pictures and maps of the countries of her origin, Ireland and Nigeria, and we were fortunate in being able to obtain some photographs through various social workers; on the first page we put a photostat copy of her original birth certificate. I also wrote to house parents from her children's home, who were delighted to send us photographs of themselves to put in her book and so help her to remember a part of her early life. Working on the book has given us both a wonderful opportunity to deepen our relationship in discussing a very intimate part of herself. Although she still would not on her own initiative talk about her past, she is proud of her scrapbook and will willingly show it to interested friends. We now feel certain that she understands why she is brown with curly hair, how she came to live in a children's home, and why she is one of the 'adopted' children in our family – leaving no room, we hope, for fantasizing.

I hope our children will always feel that we will answer any questions they may want to ask us about their origins with total honesty, and that we would be very prepared to help them find further information if we ourselves do not have the answers.

1977

- We had both our children from small babies – Anna was one week old and Matthew two weeks; it was therefore very tempting to keep the truth hidden from them. However, we had used the work 'adopted' to Anna, and had talked about being specially chosen and belonging when a friend of ours became pregnant when Anna was about three and a half years old. 'Was I in your tummy long?' she asked, and I realized the moment of truth had arrived. I explained that she came out of another lady's tummy, and how she had been given to us look after as the other lady could not do so. I deliberately did not use the term 'mother', as I believe this is too confusing at this stage. 'Do you wish I had come out of your tummy?' she said, and I assured her that I did, and that she belonged to us just as much as if she had. She was quiet after that, and the subject was dropped. However, for the following two nights we had wet beds, which had not happened before; then on the third day at breakfast she said, 'Did I come out of that lady's tummy across the road?' and I realized my mistake in not giving her her mother's Christian name. This I told her, and she was thrilled, as we had used it for her second name. Luckily, a little boy who was also adopted was coming to play that day, and I said, 'You know, James didn't come out of Mary's tummy either and he's adopted too.' When we picked James up from his home an amusing conversation ensued in the back of the car as to who had been born in the largest hospital. There was no more bedwetting; and although we have elaborated on the history as and when she has asked, I feel the biggest and most difficult step was taken then. At least, I did think so until the other day. Anna, aged seven, said, 'Emma says you're not my real mother because I didn't come out of your tummy. You are, aren't you?' Praying for the right words I said, 'I am your real mother because being a mother means loving and looking after you, not only having you in my tummy.' She was too young to go into biological details, and this seemed to satisfy her. Emma appears to have stopped taunting, so she must have given an adequate reply.

    Matthew grew up always knowing but not very interested – his realization came when he was four years old, during a conversation about our cat having a kitten which grew up to be a tom much larger than herself. 'Sons are usually taller than their mothers so maybe it's the same with cats,' I said. 'Matthew may *not* be bigger than you as he didn't come out of your tummy,' Anna interrupted, followed by a vehement denial from Matthew. The same assurances, but with a name for the mother this time, followed, and Matthew's first hard fact of life was learnt. However, there were no repercussions and he has not asked any questions – he genuinely does not appear interested.

Adoption is a fact of life in our household – we do not make a point of talking overmuch about it, neither do we hide it. We do not introduce our children as our adopted son or daughter, but equally it is a fact available quite openly if required.

1981

- Have you thought that explaning 'the adoption story' to your child could bring problems which you haven't foreseen? We started explaining about adoption and her 'first' parents to our daughter, Melanie, when she was about three years old. As she got older we went over the story again – her first mother (Avril) and father weren't married, and were not in a position to provide a home for her. One part I left out was that Avril had an older boy by an earlier marriage. I thought Melanie would understand this at a later stage.

  All was going well, with only an occasional 'reminder', until last year when she was nearly nine years old. Suddenly there was a great and urgent interest to find and see Avril. I explained this could only be done when she was 18. Flood of tears – 'Perhaps she will be dead by then!' She was really getting upset. Her feelings were very mixed. She loved us and certainly didn't want to leave home or have us upset – but she knew Avril was her 'real' mother because she had given her birth. She loved her too (even though she could not remember her). We went over the story again, explaining that mothering was not just 'giving birth', but looking after children as well, and I was doing that as well as (if not better) than mothers of her friends. Eventually, I began to wonder why birth should feature so strongly in her feelings (we were on to birth-control and abortion by now as well). Suddenly, I realized it was the sex education film she had seen at school earlier in the year – about the birth of a baby!

  We got in touch with the adoption social worker who had dealt with her case. She was very sweet and suggested she write Melanie a letter about the first part of her life. In the meantime I had to explain about Avril's other child, as this was part of the story which couldn't be left out. The letter was duly written and I saw it before it was given to Melanie. The explanations were very clear. It upset her a little, but the social worker came to see her to answer her questions. She now keeps the letter and copies of her birth certificate in a 'special file' in her room, and she feels more settled and secure again. I wonder how many other girls have had these feelings (I know at least one other) – perhaps it has to do with their sexuality!

1981

- Elizabeth came to us when she was eight, bringing with her many happy memories of her life in a nursery and children's home. Because she came with very strong feelings of anger and distrust, we found her very much more understandable than we would had she come willingly and trustingly. Because she expressed her feelings very forcefully, we have been fortunate in not being allowed to put off talking about the past with her. Elizabeth has an album of photographs dating back to the time when she was a few weeks old, and her life-story book, a sensitive account of what is known about her parents and sister, her life in care and the search for a family for her, which was made with Elizabeth by her social worker from Parents for Children in the course of her preparation for adoption. We feel strongly that unless old friendships and loyalties continue and are valued, new relationships will be expected to be transitory. Though her old children's home has closed, we have regular contact either by letter or by exchanging visits with two children who were brought up with Elizabeth, her former house mother and some of her former colleagues, her nursery nurse who has known her from when she was a few days old, her last teacher at her London primary school, and a voluntary social uncle, who has worked especially hard in keeping the children and staff in touch with each other. Elizabeth's sister has been adopted by another family, and we exchange visits several times a year.

  Elizabeth asks us questions about her mother and talks to her sister about her. Frequently she asks if her father put his 'willy' into her mother, as if seeking reassurance that she was conceived and born in the normal way and is not merely a product of the borough council. We reassure her that her mother did love her father, and did love her and wanted to keep her, but that her mother's family had many children and could not help her mother look after Elizabeth. More recently Elizabeth has asked us to agree that it's all right to have a baby at 15, because her mother did. To this we reply that it is very difficult for a girl so young to look after a baby, emphasize how unhappy her mother must have been to part with her, and say that we hope that Elizabeth will wait until she has a husband. Certainly we always try to avoid any implied criticism of her mother and her family, but we do emphasize that she is now a member of our family and that a family supports its members when they are in difficulty – this always leads to the vehement denial that she is a member of our family, but we insist that she now really is. We expect that when Elizabeth is older she will want to find her mother. We do not see this as a threat to ourselves, having emphasized the permanence of relationships, nor do we feel that by not insisting that she regards us as her family, we are letting her feel that we are being halfhearted about her adoption into our family.

1981

- It is a frequent conversation in our home that starts:
    'Well, my dad was a weight-lifter, wasn't he, Mum?'
    'Yes dear.'
    'And he was black – and so was yours, Simon.'
    'Yes, but I was born in Birmingham.'
    'Where were you born, Mum?'
  Lucy was adopted as a baby and Simon was long-term fostered; so Simon remembers well going to the judge to adopt our baby, and Lucy remembers at the age of three going to court to adopt her older brother Simon, so they talk about it between themselves. When we adopted Simon I tried to find out as much as possible from his previous foster mothers and the adoption agency about his babyhood, e.g. his weight at birth, photographs, and these are now part of an ongoing album with not only photographs but also birthday cards, certificates and pictures. We have also made an album for the other children. This puts adoption into perspective. We had done some short-term fostering, so when, four years after we had adopted Lucy, we produced a home-grown baby, there was great concern that we were not going to adopt him because 'otherwise you might give him away'. During my pregnancy I had many questions along the lines: 'Did I kick in my mum's tummy?', 'Did she breastfeed me?', 'Did I cry a lot?', and Simon said, 'I think my mum cuddled me when I was born!'
  We now have an eldest daughter from the PPIAS Newsletter, who knows very little about her early childhood, and says so whenever Lucy and Simon start discussing their natural parents. But she does visit her mother, which adds a new perspective to the discussions. None of them ever talks about

parents and origins when visitors are there, but Simon will show his album to selected visitors. With our eldest girl we made a clear chronological chart starting with her parents' marriage and including birthdays – her own and her brother's – where and when she was in care, and other significant events such as starting school. With all our children, 'telling' is about their whole lives, not just a secret past, and it goes on all the time.

1981

CHAPTER 10

Keeping in touch: adoption with contact

The previous chapter ('Telling') outlined the different ways in which adoptive parents share and, in a sense, keep alive the past for their children. Sometimes nowadays, as children are being placed for adoption when they are older and are, understandably, reluctant to relinquish all their ties with their natural family, an adoption that allows for continuing contact with the natural relatives occurs. Usually these relatives are siblings or grandparents, aunts and uncles – but sometimes they include natural parents too. For instance, contact may continue with a loving parent who is seriously ill and therefore unable to care for her child any more.

Whilst adopters may agree initially to the idea of contact with natural relatives, once they have become emotionally and psychologically attached to their child they may not find it so easy to share him with his other family. The natural relatives may find that because of their strong feelings they cannot make the contact work. And what of the child? Will he be torn between two families, unable to commit himself fully to either? It is a situation needing delicate handling but one which *can* nevertheless be productive for all the parties involved. If the adoptive family is able to 'adopt' one of their child's natural relatives, for instance a grandmother, they may find in her an additional source of support and caring. She may even have the answers to some of their queries about their child's background and behaviour. The grandmother herself, instead of feeling that she is losing her grandchild, will know that she has something to offer and, more importantly, her continuing relationship may serve as a bridge during the child's transition to his new family, ensuring that he does feel totally cut off from his earlier life. Much of the success of such a triangular relationship will depend on the personalities of those involved. The accounts which are featured in this chapter describe how some PPIAS families have fared.

Contact began with Theresa's natural family because we fostered her at first and felt that, while there was any chance of her returning to her family, we should help her keep a link with them. As we came to know them we realized they were a lovely source of caring, and that Theresa could best understand that they had always loved her by experiencing their continuing love.

We meet twice yearly and pad out the time between with letters and photos. Contact is with Theresa's mother, her grandfather, and an aunt and her husband and children. These were the people who had looked after her until we fostered her. Other relatives send Christmas cards and presents and contribute their news. One visit is just before Christmas, when we meet at a leisure centre to celebrate one of our son's and Theresa's birthdays and to exchange presents. Everyone is included in the present-giving, and our two home-grown sons receive as much in the way of fuss and presents as Theresa. We chose the leisure centre as a venue because anyone who felt shy or strained could escape to the activities of the centre. Combining a swim, a meal out, and a few games of space invaders with meeting everyone helps to make sure the day is looked forward to and talked about after. Mid-year, Theresa's family spend a day at our farm so that she can show off her room etc.

Certainly Theresa exploits the extra attention and has to be cut back to size a bit after visits, but she does gain more than a pile of presents and a loaded moneybox, and she is beginning to see that it is love she is receiving. We have adopted Theresa now, and it was because her natural family could see what we were giving her that they cooperated in every way they could to help through the adoption process. We all felt we pulled together to do what was right for her. She won't ever need to wonder about her roots, because they are continuing alongside her adopted family. She does need to know, however, that she is a part of her new family and stays with us through the bad and the good patches. Any question of switching to her natural family is definitely out.

Theresa's natural family have always said they would drop out of her life if we felt that was right for her. This and their undoubted love was our assurance that we should make sure she had access to their love. We would never have maintained contact for contact's sake, nor for the sake of her natural family, however much we felt for them – it had to be for Theresa. As it has turned out, we have all gained.

1983

Keeping in touch: adoption with contact

- About two years ago we took into our family Sarah, a mentally handicapped girl, then aged 12. Sarah had lived in a children's home nearly all her life, but her grandparents had always manintained close contact with her. They visited her once a week and had her at their home for part of every school holiday. Through her visits to them she had some contact with aunts, uncles and cousins, though no recent contact with her mother. In her own interests, therefore, it was felt that contact with her grandparents must continue, though geographical distance would, in any case, necessitate its becoming less frequent. We were introduced to the grandparents at their home shortly after our first few visits to Sarah. We liked them, and they fortunately liked us, and approved of the plan for Sarah's future.

We were initially a bit apprehensive as to how Sarah would bond with our family when she still had her own family connections. We need not have worried. She readily accepted our family as hers, without any rejection of her own. Her grandparents come to stay with us for the occasional weekend, and she goes to stay with them for about one week, twice a year. In addition we make weekly phone calls to each other. Her contact

Sarah with her adoptive parents Michael and Margaret (left) and natural grandparents.

with our own near relatives follows a similar pattern, and she is as happy staying with them as with her own. Perhaps being mentally handicapped has helped her to accept both families on equal terms, but we should emphasize that she is not emotionally shallow – indeed, she is a child with very strong feelings, is fully aware of her past, and takes as much interest in it as any normal person. We feel that we, as well as Sarah, have benefited and indeed continue to benefit from the contact with her grandparents. They are supportive, and when one takes a mentally handicapped child, one needs support from others.

1983

- 'They're here – they're here – they've got a red car and they're here,' Paul and Jane rushed in to tell us. As they hadn't seen their older brother and sister for nearly two years, it was hardly surprising that the excitement was so great. The four children had all been placed in care together, the youngest when only a few months old. They finally ended up in a children's home. The older two, Tom and Clare, at seven and six, had left the home to be adopted by a childless couple in the midlands. Both Tom and Clare and their new parents had felt guilty and anxious about leaving behind the younger two. Paul and Jane, aged five and four, came to live with us in the south of England about a year later. While all four children were settling in, both parents and social workers alike felt that contact at that stage should be limited to exchanging letters, photos and cards. Paul and Jane were almost too busy settling into a large family to notice that natural siblings were missing, although we could tell from Tom and Clare's letters that the anxiety level was still high.

And so the first visit was arranged. The four children eyed each other in wonder and amazement and then all rushed round the garden madly spraying each other with a hose pipe – with all their clothes on! Since that visit Tom and Clare and their family, which now includes a toddler, have come down south for four more visits – the first two were spent camping, and the second two in our home.

The effect of the contact on the two pairs of children has been interesting. From our side of the picture we have always felt that the older children have needed the contact more – although Jane was extremely upset when one visit had to be cancelled due to bad health. The older two children are very protective towards the younger two when together. Tom particularly remembers the times when they were still all together, and has filled us in with some details of Paul and Jane's early life. Tom, too, is still the leader of the group when they are together; and all four children obviously benefit from being together from time to time, and look back on the holidays as being good times. Our natural and other adopted children seem to have taken the visits in their stride. Tom and Clare's parents have been particularly good at showing an interest in all our family, which has prevented any resentment or jealousy.

As to the future – Tom and Clare and their family have now moved to an island off Scotland, so contact will be more limited in the future. However, all four adoptive parents feel that the link has been made and kept, and that in the future the children as older teenagers will think nothing of travelling a few hundred miles to see each other.

1983

- Alison was five when she came to us. The first three years she had been in and out of care because of her mother's alcoholism, and then the next two years were spent in a nursery with mother visiting weekly. Because of her mother's needs and her difficult personality, a foster home was sought that could tolerate her mother and an enhanced rate was to be paid.

    It was decided when Alison came to us that visits should be set at two-weekly intervals, and that they should be in a neutral place. My husband and I took responsibility for alternate visits, and the social worker took Alison for the other visits. None of us looked forward to these meetings; but after a year I felt I could tolerate having the visits in my home, and consequently Alison's mother came to my home once a fortnight. Alison was always pleased to see her and she liked visiting. However, after about a year I began to feel the strain, as her mother would never leave the house unless I practically pushed her out of the door, and I began to dread each visit. By this time there had been two changes of social worker: our support began to dwindle, and I felt I was being left to handle the situation on my own. A case conference was then held, at which it was decided that Alison needed to know what her permanent future would be, as for two years she had been trying to settle with us while at the same time having her mother constantly telling her that in a few months she would be having her back. Secondly, because of the strain I was under, for the next few visits the social worker was intending to be present.

    Alison's mother was extremely resentful at the proposition

that a social worker should be present, and a couple of nasty scenes took place in my house, with Alison anxiously dancing up and down, not knowing what to do about it. Then her mother disappeared for a while as she went on a drinking episode. After that it was decided that I should take Alison to the social services office and the social worker would completely supervise the visits. Alison herself was frightened to be with her mother on her own because her mother would, despite our warnings, take her to a public house and get drunk, bringing back for Alison all her earlier memories and fears.

Alison's mother became furious at having to have the social worker present and used to abuse him verbally, making each meeting an ordeal for both him and, of course, Alison. After the last meeting, when the mother made a terrible scene in public, spitting at the social worker, he refused to supervise any more visits. At this point also Alison's mother was rapidly going downhill. Hospitals were refusing to tolerate her, and she was admitted to hospital a couple of times, under intensive care. At this point, much to everyone's relief, her father came over from Ireland and took her back. She has been in a mental hospital ever since, and her only contact with Alison is by letter. Five years have now gone by and we have decided that it is the right thing for Alison that she be adopted by us. She wants this, and so do the other children in our family. A neutral social worker has been involved to explore Alison's feelings and wishes, and to prepare the ground for adoption.

We hope to adopt this year, but we realize there is going to be a battle and we are not looking forward to it. We feel very sad for Alison's mother, who loses the one person she feels is 'hers', but Alison must come first. I am not sure about contact after adoption. I think that if the adoption goes through perhaps a letter once a year would suffice. The fostering social worker who originally placed her said that, in retrospect, Alison ought to have been placed straight for adoption five years ago, when it was clearly seen that rehabilitation would not work. I feel she is right. The longer things go on, the harder it gets for natural parent, adoptive parent and child.

1983

- This meeting, of all of them, was the one we feared most. A miserable rainy day in the park with our neighbours as chaperones. We told our children we were going on a picnic to see 'someone they used to live with'. That someone was their natural mother Jill, and we, their prospective adoptive parents, were terrified. Would the children reject us when they saw Jill? Would they be upset? Would she snatch them back? What transpired was a frail, sad meeting where Jill helped to cement the four of us into a family. Our fears had not come true. What we had not anticipated were our feelings of pity and gratitude.

We first met our adopted children when they were living with their natural mother. The meeting was in a stark social services office with two toys, four seats and a social worker as embarrassed as we were. There they played; Sally at 18 months, Graham at 2¾ years and their mother at 20 years. Graham knew something was up and hid behind a chair, but Sally was more approachable. Jill was coolly appraising us and the children's reaction to us. How do you prepare for this moment? You are asked to go, view and take an option on some children and their mother. Jill had put the children into voluntary care and up for adoption, with the proviso that she should meet and approve of the prospective adopters and continue to see the children after adoption.

Jill is an uneducated but attractive, capable girl whom our (and her) daughter Sally closely resembles physically. Wilful like Sally, Jill resolutely failed to attend any meeting on time. However, she did always turn up, breathless, usually in a taxi, Graham and Sally clutching their overnight bags and toys and with us peering through the window wondering if the whole thing had fallen through. Jill would stay and stay and stay: eating cake, watching television and talking about the children. There she sat and we sat; our children's mother and her children's prospective parents talking small talk. The rules of polite society do not provide for this situation. She coped magnificently while we skirted around the awkward areas, and then Jill went off to a disco. The next morning or (gradually) the following afternoon or weekend, she would return to take the children back. One day it was agreed she would not come back to pick them up, and she didn't.

For the next two years we fostered the children and during this time we (in the absence of Graham and Sally) met Jill on a number of occasions. We learned more about the children but never came very close to Jill. Which brings us back to the rainy day in the park. The day before we went to court, Jill wanted to see the children again. She had not seen them for two years and did not wish to see them for another two years. Graham, again, knew something was up and hid behind a park bench, and Sally was more approachable. With sadness and relief we noted two years had changed their relationship with us and with Jill.

Jill came with us to court. After the adoption order was made, her social worker, the guardian ad litem, we and our lawyer all had a tearful final tea-party. We do not know whether Jill will take up her right of access in two years' time. The frequency of access after the two years will be at our discretion. In spite of two years' experience in meeting with Jill, we are no better prepared for the future encounters. Will it go as well as the day in the park?

Are there any messages from our experience in meeting the natural parent? We found the following useful:

Meet on neutral ground.

If it appears natural, try to have a third party present.

Have an informal (unwritten) agenda of what you want to get out of the meeting (in your own mind).

Set a time to begin and end.

Do not expect too much intimacy – at the end of the day your only common link may be the children.

1983

CHAPTER 11

Tracing

The Children's Act 1975 (section 26) gave the adopted person over the age of 18 the right of access to his original birth records. It added the provision that anyone adopted before the Act came into force must receive counselling from a social worker before the information could be made available to him.
Counselling for those adopted after the Act came into force is optional. Once he has received his original birth records and been counselled by a social worker, if this is required, the adopted person may then, if he chooses, try to trace his natural parents. He – and only he – may take the initiative: the most that a natural father or mother can do is to send a letter to the Registrar General, in the hope that one day their child may make an application under section 26.

Only a very small percentage of adopted persons decide to trace their natural family. Most of those who do are mature adults in their late 20s or 30s, well adjusted and successful members of society. According to the Post-Adoption Center for Education and Research in California (PACER), adoptees who decide to trace have not usually had unhappy adoptive experiences. If this is the case, what is it that gives rise to a need to trace?

Chapter 9 ('Telling') stressed how important it is for adopters to give their children all the information they have about their origins. The more positive information they can give, the less likely it may be that their children will want to search out their natural parents. But, as the accounts in this chapter describe, there is a very deepseated need in some adoptees, something more than curiosity, which will lead a few to pursue their search until *all* their questions are answered. And most evidence shows that, however the search ends, few people have regretted tracing. It has usually 'put their minds at rest'.

- A question commonly asked of adopted people is, 'How did you feel when you found out you were adopted?' It is a question I cannot answer. I never 'found out' I was adopted, it was just a fact I had known all my life. I must have been told of my adoption by the time I was three years old, and simply grew up with the knowledge, treating it in the same way as the fact I had eczema as a baby. I was greatly loved, wanted and, as I was keen to tell playground adversaries, chosen. I was told I was adopted as the lady I was born to was unable to look after me. As only illness ever prevented mummy from looking after me, I assumed my natural mother had been ill. I equated illness with old age, and throughout my childhood visualized Rose, my natural mother, as a small, bent, old lady in a grey coat and felt hat.

During the turbulent teenage years it is easy to seek a cause for the problems that befall every family. Adoption is an obvious scapegoat. There was, however, a short period when I was desperately aware that I had only been available to be chosen because someone had not wanted me. Soon there were parties to attend, boyfriends to weep over, and Rose remained a shadowy background figure. Until last year I only thought about Rose on the day my first child was born. Only adopted people can appreciate how it feels 20 or more years to see the first person ever to whom you are truly related. As I cuddled my baby son I was aware that I could not possibly envisage any circumstances capable of parting me from William. I then realized what terrible pressures and anguish Rose must have suffered.

In November 1975 the Children's Act became law, giving adoptees over the age of eighteen the right of access to their original birth records. There was considerable public concern and media publicity about this provision, but it all passed over me. I was more concerned about escalating mortgage rates and soaring energy prices to notice. This perhaps illustrates that awareness only comes when one is ready. In the autumn of 1981 a plethora of unconnected events contrived to bring Rose to the forefront of my mind; articles on genealogy, doctors' questions about hereditary complaints, and not least William. Now seven and a half, he was becoming an intensified mirror image of myself, temperamental and absent-minded; we were constantly meeting in head-on conflict from which we were both too strong-willed to withdraw. I could only understand William better if I knew more about myself, and the key to that knowledge was Rose.

Tracing Rose was remarkably easy. She now lives less than a mile from the address given on my birth certificate. A quick telephone call to an old neighbour and a search of old and the current electoral registers soon revealed all. I spent an interesting day at St Catherine's House checking all the details I had discovered (with this type of inquiry it is impossible to be too sure of anything), and found that the younger of her two subsequent daughters had recently married. Rose lived in a northern seaside town; in February I went with my family to stay there for a weekend. In the library I searched old local papers to see if my halfsister's wedding was featured. I thought I was looking for a name, but suddenly I turned the page, and staring up at me was the 'twin' of my own wedding photograph. There was no doubt I had found the right family!

As Rose was a teacher I assumed she might be first home each afternoon. I parked my car outside her house at 3.15, but it soon became obvious that there was already someone indoors. At 3.30 an 'arty' girl of around 28 came out and drove away. I was pleased, as I anticipated Rose's return to the empty house. How wrong I was. Ten minutes later the girl returned with Rose; she had been providing a taxi service for her mother – my mother. I was almost obstructing their driveway, but they were so deep in conversation they did not notice me; unreasonably that hurt me badly. Part of me wanted to leap from my car and shout 'Look at me, I'm here' whilst my more realistic side said 'go home, forget it.' I compromised. From a telephone box I called Rose. I explained who I was and that I had come a long way to see her. Although shocked, she agreed to come to our hotel that evening.

At 6.30 I was waiting but sure she would not come; by 6.45 I was convinced she would not; at 6.50 there was a knock on the door. She walked into the room and held out her arms to me; we held each other tightly for several minutes in that electric atmosphere. Then we talked and talked about her family and mine and studied photographs of both. She had not spent the time since my call dressing up for the occasion but, generously, in searching out old photographs and press cuttings she thought might interest me. To my query about William's temperament she laughed. 'My dear, he comes from a very temperamental family.' I too could laugh, for now I knew someone else had coped with the problem and I could cope as well. She came for an hour and stayed three. We write to each other and she is a light in my life. Her husband has always been aware of me, although her daughters are not, but one day, who knows?
1984

- My adoptive parents did a very good job of bringing up a family. They also adopted a girl, a younger sister for me, who has always been perfectly happy with her situation, never, even now, having the slightest desire to know more about her natural parents. We both knew the fact of our adoption from our earliest days. My yearning began with the 'identity crisis' which often comes with adolescence even without adoption. I resented being different from everybody else. All my life, until six months ago, I always felt deprived whenever I heard people talking of their family trees or of where their ancestors were buried or what they did. Although I was fond of my grandparents, and had aunts and uncles who meant all the exciting things aunts and uncles are supposed to, as a young adult I felt out of it whenever there was talk of my adoptive family's forebears and places of origin, as there will inevitably be from time to time in any family. I knew that they weren't 'mine', and felt I had nothing but a total vacuum. All this with the most loving and sensible parents, wise in their handling of the adoption situation.

  It might have been better if my aptitudes and interests had coincided more with those of my adoptive father. I think that more care is taken these days, but, when it was known that my own father and my mother's brother were engineers, it does seem unwise to have placed me with a man who admits he has no technical interests or abilities whatever. I know that many natural sons feel different from their fathers, but as I grew up it became apparent that my interests, abilities and personality did not match in any way those of the rest of the family. I can see that my sister fits in far better. She is an easy-going and happy person. She says herself, in discussing this with me, that I am 'a complex personality' and that, once I grew up, she and our parents realized that I was anxious about being adopted since I never mentioned the subject, even changing the subject rapidly if it ever came up.

  Now that I know who I am, I feel equal to everybody else. Friends and colleagues who know nothing of what I have been doing have commented that I have changed, becoming more relaxed and happy. I have seen the grave of my great-grandparents and grandfather. I have discovered more about them than my mother and her family ever knew, to their surprise. I can see something of myself in many of the photographs I have seen. Before, I had to make do with a fantasy brother. I now discover that it is not unknown for a child to invent a fantasy sibling who is like him in every way, but it had led me to wonder whether I had a twin, separated on adoption, even at times becoming convinced that I must have had.

Whether giving me more information in my teens would have helped, I do not know. What I had was so pathetically sparse – about three sentences in a letter from the adoption society at the time – that when I first saw it at 14, all it did was to excite curiosity without telling enough to satisfy it. It may be that I would have been far happier without ever having seen it, but I doubt it. I doubt also whether much fuller information would have satisfied the need to know. It would probably have fed the desire by giving something more concrete to fasten on. As it was, I was left tantalized, and remained so for more than 30 years, although it stayed mostly in the background, not often coming to the surface.

What finally impelled me to do something was the knowledge that if I left it much longer it would be too late. I was inhibited from doing anything for years by factors which are quite common: I had feelings of guilt, partly connected with a desire not to hurt adoptive parents while they were still alive, but also arising from the impression that society was against the enterprise, regarding it as perverse and indecent to harbour such a desire, and until recently, backing that belief legally: I did not know that the search was at all a feasible proposition and so feared to start in case the trail went cold, leaving me with the certainty of never knowing:

And, curiously, I imagined having to give an account of myself, as though to St Peter, when I succeeded. In fact my adoptive parents have been very understanding, saying that they have long thought I might do this. It has brought me closer to them, and I have been able to talk appreciatively about our relationship. My own teenage children fully understand that this in no way alters the relationship between them and their loving grandparents. It is a pity that, as having all this in the open is so beneficial now, inhibitions, or whatever, prevented free discussion over all those years. It brings home the oft-heard advice to all parents that their children should always feel they can dicuss with them their worries and problems – easier said than done, I fear.

The realization of how much like me my elder daughter is, particularly in the way she thinks, was one of the spurs which finally started me on the trail, especially after my wife, in replying to my marvelling at the resemblance, observed that I had never before known a blood relative. Another pressure was a reluctance to see my children deprived of their ancestors in the way that I had been, even if only on one side of the family in their case. Not wanting them to feel different from others in the way that I had, even slightly, was one of the things that had kept me from telling them that I was adopted. They now show wonderful understanding of the whole situation.

I know that times have changed since my day, but people and their emotions do not change. It would be a pity if old misunderstandings of adopted people's feelings were to be repeated, in particular society's belief that the break could or should be total and forever. Some of us, like my sister, are perfectly happy with that, but others have a real need, which has been cruelly denied in the past. I suspect that many adopters think of this as an unpleasant spectre which, if ignored, will go away; or as merely curiosity, easily satisfied with an information pack. I dare say some young people do have curiosity which goes no deeper, and I am sure that curiosity is a totally insuffficient reason for embarking on a course which can lead to great upset for all concerned; but if your child turns out to be like me, he or she will respect you greatly for your understanding of something which is deeper than curiosity.

1984

- At four months old I was placed with my adoptive family whilst my twin brother, Colin, remained in care, owing to his ill-health and to doubts, at the time, over his survival. I knew from a very early age that I was adopted and that I had a twin brother; I admired my parents for their enlightened attitude (this was in the early 1950s) and appreciated their honesty. The only problem was that, because I knew of my brother's existence, I also knew that I would like to find him.

My first attempt to trace Colin was when I was 16 years old, just before my adoptive mother died, and I gave up the search before I had really started, feeling that my actions might be misinterpreted as a search for my original mother, in whom I actually had no interest.

It was nearly 20 years later that I was able, with the help of a social worker researching into twins, to make contact with Colin (although it had been very much on my mind for many years prior to this). His initial reaction, a contact from the social worker, was to refuse to see me and to reject my existence. I found this surprising, but now believe his reluctance had much to do with the fact that his eventual adoptive placement was a failure and he had to return into care. I feel that he did not wish to relive his bad experiences or rekindle his feelings about the past. His life looks forward to the future with his wife and two children. However, within a relatively short time he had written to me and sent me a photograph – which was mind-blowing; the resemblance between us was amazing.

We have only had one meeting, one day in London in 1982, both of us having to travel long distances to meet. It was an incredible, shattering experience; I was awake from 4 o'clock in the morning, worrying, and I stood at the railway station with shaking legs, terrified. I recognized Colin immediately and he recognised me, but we just stood and stared dumbfounded until his wife stepped forward and introduced us! I gather that his initial feelings of terror, excitement and amazement were very like mine, but above all I felt fulfilled – part of myself had been returned.

I had been warned by the social worker not to expect too much from this meeting and I did not expect an instant, wonderful family to rush forward to embrace me, because I knew we had spend 36 years leading our own lives and growing apart. I hope that we will start growing together as the years pass, and I do have the satisfaction of knowing that we belong to one another and of knowing he is always there. However, I do not foresee that we will ever become very close. Too much has happened in between to mould us into very different people with very different views on life (although incredibly the same physically).

I would say to people who want to make this sort of contact: don't forget that whoever it is you are looking for has had his or her own life, a complete and total life which never included you, and although he or she may be ready to welcome you into that life you really have to discover each other again totally.

1984

● The tracing was easy. My natural family had kept in contact with the firm of solicitors who had handled my adoption. Within five weeks letters had been exchanged. My natural parents had married each other after my adoption had taken place, and I had a brother and a sister! They lived in America. A meeting was set up. I was going to go to America with a friend anyway, and we had planned to travel from Los Angeles to New York. My natural family lived in Florida, so it seemed ideal to meet them after the arranged trip. Unfortunately my natural father could not understand why I was taking so long in arriving. One morning I was woken up and told that my father was on the telephone . . . . it was not the father I was expecting to hear from. This strange voice boomed down the line announcing himself as my father. Within minutes he was offering to get me a 'green card' so I could live and work in the States if I wanted to. It made me even more apprehensive about the forthcoming meeting. At 21 I felt rather independent, and certainly had no intention of settling into my natural family's home. About a month later my friend and I were in Indiana. I was given a message that my mother had telephoned ... I was suddenly faced with a problem – I did not know which one. To this day friends can get confused about which mother I am talking about! That week I spoke to my natural mother and brother; they did not seem nearly as demanding as my natural father, so I felt a little easier about meeting them all.

The actual meeting took place at Fort Lauderdale airport. I do not remember much, but I think we shook hands! I felt very isolated in their home, with strangers who were my 'natural' family. Looking back, I think it would have been easier if we had met on neutral ground. My 'sister' hardly spoke to me. She recently told me that she had only known about me that year and had resented this 'stranger' soaking up all the attention in the house. She withdrew from me and her parents. Somehow I could cope better with my sister's rejection than all the 'family' friends who wanted to meet me. I have lost count how many times I had to tell my side of the story, and how I felt about meeting my 'natural' family. It must have been difficult for my sister: she, being the youngest, had enjoyed all the attention, while her brother was in college in Canada. I had known that I was adopted from the age of two, so finding out that I had a sister was, for me, very exciting; while, to her, I must have seemed quite a threat.

The 'family' were going to spend some time at their holiday home on the Caribbean island where my natural father was born. They suggested I join them, with a view to getting to know each other. During the holiday, my 'brother' spent a lot of his time with his girlfriend, and my 'sister' was still treating me as a stranger. So, after three weeks, we still had not become any closer. There was so much to ask my 'parents', but I often felt awkward around them. However, they introduced me, unashamedly, as their daughter – to both relatives and friends. My 'mother' found it hard to talk about the adoption, and her guilt at giving me up was deepened by the fact that my adoptive parents had divorced when I was ten – both had subsequently remarried. My 'father' was nothing like the daunting prospect I thought I would meet, but if I wanted it he probably would still get me a green card!

My adoptive mother and her husband joined us on holiday for two weeks. Having two mothers in the same house was unsettling. There was my mum, who had brought me up, a mum in every sense of the word. Then there was my natural mother, a woman I had only met four weeks before. I looked like she did and recognized parts of myself in her; it was very disconcerting. We had some laughs though. At parties, my natural mother would introduce us. 'This is my daughter . . . and this is her mother.' These bewildered faces just stared back, trying to work it out! After my mum and her husband returned to England, my natural parents and I flew to a neighbouring island for a few days to meet my (adoptive) father and his wife, who were on holiday there. My triangle was now complete.

I am very fortunate that both sets of parents were keen to meet and have continued to see each other. Having said that, after the final meeting, I was not too sad to leave them all behind and make my way to Australia. Eight months there enabled me to 'recover' and work out, uninfluenced by any one parent, where I fitted into this ever-expanding family! Sometimes I feel I do not fit in with any of them – it's very confusing seeing aspects of oneself in so many people.

That was four years ago. I see my natural family once or twice a year. They spend their summers in London, where I live. I get along a lot better now with my natural brother and sister, but my relationship with them will never be the same as the one I share with the two brothers from my adoptive family, as we grew up together. Although my new brother, sister and I are the children of the same parents and we have many of the same family characteristics, our attitudes are very different. Maybe we can all accept this and become closer; but there is the question whether, if we were not blood-related, we would still want to see each other. My natural parents have been kind and generous ever since I met them. At times they try to influence me – as if they are forgetting that I am already living my own life.

Although I had been well prepared by family, friends and the media for what could go wrong, and I have been exceptionally lucky in how everything has turned out, I still was not prepared for the responsibility and demands a natural family can make.

1984

CHAPTER 12

Transracial adoption

Transracial adoption — the placing of a child of one racial origin (usually black or of mixed parentage) in a family of a different origin (usually white) — began to flourish in this country in the mid-1960s and reached a peak in the mid-1970s. Nowadays the aim of agencies is to place black children with black families wherever possible.

One of the criticisms by the black community of transracial adoption is that black babies were *only* placed with white couples in this country when the supply of white babies had begun to dwindle. In retrospect, it is clear that more efforts should have been made earlier to recruit adopters for black children — especially black adopters. Certainly, since its launch in 1980, John Small's New Black Families Project has proved that it is possible to find parents from the black community for children needing permanent new families. The project accepts that there are many different styles of life and ways of bringing up children. Some of the black couples who have been approved by the unit have been older than is the norm for adopters; sometimes both parents have been working full-time. Now that more agencies are taking this more flexible approach to family finding, there is hope that same-race placements will be possible for all black children needing permanent new families in the future.

But what of those mixed-race families already created by transracial adoption? How have they fared? A major concern of black social workers is that white families have neither the experience nor the capacity to equip a black child to deal with racial prejudice. They fear that white parents cannot make a black child feel proud of his race, nor give him adequate opportunity to mix with other black children and adults. He will be 'black on the outside but white in the middle'. These fears are largely upheld by the findings of the most recent research project on the subject by Owen Gill and Barbara Jackson.* They interviewed a

---

* Adoption and Race: Black, Asian and Mixed-race Children in White Families (London, Batsford, 1983).

Transracial adoption

sample of black teenagers adopted as babies into white families in the 1960s. In general, they found that the white adoptive parents had not tried very hard to develop their black children's sense of racial identity: they were living in predominantly white areas with little contact with other black people. The adopters had, however, succeeded in integrating the children into their families, and the children themselves were happy and confident individuals. If there is a lesson to be learned from these findings, it must surely be that white adopters *can* provide a secure and loving environment for black children to grow up in, but that they must not be complacent. They will have to work at preparing their children for the prejudice they are likely to meet. If they are not living in a multiracial area, they may have to look for opportunities for contact with black people.

The accounts written by PPIAS families in this chapter reflect the changing attitudes to transracial adoption over the years. The first five accounts, written in the 1970s, reveal the families' concern with combating prejudice, and touch upon developing their children's sense of racial pride; those written after the publication of Gill and Jackson's book in 1983 are more reflective and analytical, showing a new awareness of how other people actually perceive their children. They may also sound defensive. Clearly the debate about transracial adoption is likely to continue for some time to come. If it has made white adopters more aware of the needs of their black children, it is a debate we should welcome.

Adoption: the inside story

- We named our adopted daughter Rebecca, partly because we felt that it suited her dark looks – she is half-Indian and half-Welsh. It has been a family joke for years that she should have been named April, as sunshine and showers, alternating with often startling swiftness, are very much the pattern of her life. Quite frequently the showery patches are brought on by everyday minor upsets, such as the normal teasing that any sister has to put up with when she has three bigger brothers – especially from the eldest, who very vocally despises anything female! Sometimes, though, the tears have more serious causes – such as another child being unpleasant to her about her colour. She is not at all dark really, and would pass for 'white' in a crowd in winter if you don't look too closely at fingertips, etc. Even in summer, when she tans rapidly to a darker shade of coffee, people who don't know us often comment on her beautiful tan without realizing the cause. Of course, we have talked about her adoption and her racial origins quite openly ever since she can remember, and she will happily tell anyone that she is half-Indian, but even so she still seems to get a nasty shock when someone taunts her with the fact that she is slightly different in colour to them. At eight years old, conforming is sometimes all-important, and if the image that looks at you from your mirror is virtually the same as that of all the other girls in the class, you can kid yourself that it *is* actually the same. It often seems to us that it must be easier in some ways for a much darker child to accept that she is different, because it is so much more obvious.

  We went through a bad patch in infant school, when there were tears every day as soon as she came out of school because one particular child was being unpleasant and calling her names. The school were most helpful and sympathetic, and after a couple of weeks it all died down. To any parent faced with similar problems I would say: 'Go to the school and ask them to help; don't sit and worry at home on your own.'

  Now, when Rebecca is halfway through junior school, we have just had another difficult patch. A delightful child has, among other things, been using the art period to colour little dark-brown girls and labelling them 'Rebecca'. 'But Mummy, I'm pale coffee colour, not that dark brown, aren't I?' has been the sort of problem to sort out over drinks and biscuits at homecoming. Once again, a word in the teacher's ear to let him know what has been happening has been helpful. At the moment, all is peaceful. Well, with four children that isn't meant to be taken literally! What of the future? We hope that, as she matures,

Rebecca will be able to hide the fact that she is hurt by personal remarks. Not reacting is such a good way to shut people up – but she hasn't learned that lesson yet, although we keep suggesting she tries it.

1973

- Teasing and name-calling seem to fall into roughly two categories: the sort which is cheerful, rude badinage, and the sort which is meant to hurt. We've found that the best way to handle the first is to use it sometimes within the family – as joking endearments! 'Skinny-ma-link', 'Fuzz-buzz', 'Chocolate-button', 'Paddy'! So that if faced with a shout of 'Hi, chocolate-face!' our brown-skinned children can retort, 'Vanilla-face yourself!' without anyone feeling too offended or over-sensitive. The second sort of teasing is far harder to handle. The two things which we hope will help our children not to feel too hurt are, first, to be aware beforehand of some people's prejudices and, secondly to have a very secure knowledge about their own life history and background. There just *are* people who don't like brown skins; bastardy used to be a stigma, and it does help to know that lots of other people have to suffer cruel remarks

The Chambers family: from left to right, David, Zachary, Lucy, Celia, Helen, Hilary and Judith.

('fatty', 'swot', 'carrots' or 'four-eyes') and not just those who are adopted or who happen to be black.

We hope that our children will be much less bewildered and surprised by this sort of hostility if they are very sure of the fact that they are deeply loved by their own family and circle of friends; and sure also of the facts that many people *do* have two sets of parents (what about divorce, remarriage etc?) as well as that brown-skinned people are as clever or as ordinary, as clean or as dirty, as wise or as stupid, as anyone else in the world! Ignorant and curious questions (although often hard to take) simply have to be answered straight: 'I'm adopted', 'Of course I love my adopted brother/sister as much as the others', 'No, he didn't come from Biafra – he was born in Birmingham!' One of our daughters pointed out that the questions she'd been faced with weren't intended to be hostile or pitying, but that her friends didn't have the opportunity first-hand in their own families to think about adoption, so they genuinely learned quite a lot from just knowing us!

1977

- Jane didn't understand when a child at school called her a 'wog'. As she is Anglo-Indian, it was explained that the name-caller had his 'ethnic origins' confused. Jane practised saying 'ethnic origins', which kept coming out as 'ethnic oranges', and couldn't wait to get back to school to deliver this message. The following day she raced home from school, 'Mum, he called me a "wog" again!' I asked what she'd replied. 'I forgot what you said, so I called him a snowdrop and he went away!'

- We have been concerned about the lack of understanding amongst some adults, who totally accept that our 'white' adopted daughter is unquestionably 'our' child, but do not seem to realize that this also applies to our mixed-race daughter. We get comments such as: 'Is the little coloured girl still with you?' 'Do her parents come and visit her?' or 'I wasn't sure which daddy she was referring to', as though people are confused by adoption and unable to conceive that the same conditions of adoption apply to both our children; in other words, they see her as a foster child. She finds it most irritating to have to cope with the passers-by who touch her hair or comment, 'What lovely curls you have, can you spare me one?' or 'I wish I had hair like yours', when one knows perfectly well that they wish no such thing, but cannot help commenting on the most obvious difference.

1977

- Our son was available for adoption from his birth, but we did not find him till he was six months old. He came to live with us when he was nine months old, so he has no memory of a life without us – at least, no conscious memory. His home is a big shabby house in a big shabby garden on the edge of a small village. When he was four and a half we went to Liberia on a UN assignment, and he did not go to the local primary school until he was five and a half. On being asked by other children, 'Why are you so brown?' he replied that he had been in a hot country and was very sunburnt.

We were sure, when he repeated his answer to us, that in fact he was asking us a question: that though he had very early been told he was adopted, born not to me but to another woman, he had not grasped the implications, and was confused about his colour and his black curly hair. We felt it was time, young as he was, timid and dependent as he was, for a fuller explanation of his origins. We told him that his married West Indian father had had to go back to his family, that his mother had been too young to earn her living and care for him as well. Both at this time and later, whenever the subject came up, we stressed our admiration for his father's drive and courage in making his way to this country, and for his mother's unselfishness in letting us have him. We kept silent about his mother's family's rejection of him; perhaps this silence was unwise, but he seemed to us too young and sensitive to have to accept his colour as a burden or a handicap; we wanted it to be a source of pride to him.

Outside the village and the school, he has several times met with rudeness and unkindness. With someone of his own age he will counter 'nigger' or 'jungle bunny' by 'white slug' fairly equably, but when an adult says, 'Bugger off, Sambo' he is shocked and silent. He takes a long time to recover from incidents like these; though few, they have tended to make him less outgoing and adventurous than he might otherwise have been. He doesn't like walking or going in buses and trains alone; we realize that he needs practice in this, but our circumstances make it difficult to provide, except in a very artificial way.

Children are all different; they will learn to face their problems in different ways, according to their circumstances and temperament. I'm bound to say that I think defects of character are often aggravated by colour: the aggressive child becoming more aggressive, the timid child more timid. I don't think that being the only black child in a white community is necessarily a bad thing; at any rate he can never be part of a threatening teenage gang, and so stands a better chance of being liked and accepted for himself. It may be that the white community will be a real help and support to him as he grows up. Lay the foundations of understanding early, support him by example in your attitude to any other coloured people you may meet, and by your open expression of love for him and delight in his looks. Don't say, 'It doesn't matter that you're black'; that is neither true nor positive enough – too much like the missionary's remark that in God's eyes all children are white! As he grows older, if he wants to keep his thoughts and problems to himself, respect his privacy as you would that of your 'born' child. Do not make him the object of a crusade, however worthy; he will think you adopted him for that and not because you loved him. He is not a cause, he is a person. I think you will find that the very fact of being his parent will give you an insight into what it is like to be coloured in this country that will have a lasting effect on your life and thought.

1977

- We were relieved when the transracial adoption debate came to the fore a few months ago – from the outset of our experience as transracial adopters we were very dismayed by the attitudes of the majority of white adopters with black children. In frequent discussions we seemed to be almost the sole supporters of a positive antiracist approach to bringing up children, and we now feel we can say that it does work. Arnold came to us feeling very vulnerable and ashamed about his black identity and wanting to disassociate himself from it; he is now positively proud of his colour and racial ancestry and culture, and no longer doubts that racism is evil and unfounded. So, how did this very significant change in his attitude come about in a year?

We feel that it all comes down to the deepseated feelings of the adoptive parents. Most white people are scared to face the powerful reality of racism and try to deny it; and of course for white adopters this is even more threatening, and they deny it even more hotly. Yet all white people have been brought up with a tacit (and often voiced) theory that white people are superior to all the coloured races of the world: this is there in even the most liberal of us – we ourselves have had to look honestly into our own subconscious attitudes and feelings. Children are enormously sensitive to the true feelings of adults, and so will know immediately if your interest in racial issues is not genuine. If you have any doubts, then they will not take on an image of themselves as black because they will not feel secure about it – this I think is why so many children 'reject' their parents' attempts to interest them in black culture. They will also react negatively if it is not approached in a 'whole family' perspective but as an issue of concern to them alone – they already feel anxious enough about being the odd ones out.

If you have chosen to become a transracial family you need to expand your consciousness to see life from a global perspective. You have the exciting opportunity to find a way across the divide into the other cultures around you, but you cannot be insular. You will have to face up to the appalling exploitation, past and present, of the coloured peoples of the world by the white. You will often find that questions about other countries and cultures come back to this, and you must not be afraid to join your child in his anger and experience shame yourself. Encourage your child to unburden himself by telling you about the racial abuse he encounters in the street and at school – we have been astounded by the level of abuse our son suffers, though he kept quiet about if for a long time.

The black culture will have to have a significant, if not dominant, place in your family perspective because every other influence will be portraying and reinforcing the white culture. A token attempt with a few books and the occasional embarrassed conversation will not combat it. Think how it feels to be a black child looking at books, ads, films, TV, and hardly ever seeing a similar face: the message that comes across is that there is no place for black people in our society. You will need all the information you can get if your children are to have more than a hazy image to hold up against the wall of insults and ignorance they will encounter. Make sure that your home reflects your multicultural identity with posters, postcards, items from other countries, black dolls, books, etc.

We hope this does not seem a weighty and difficult task, because for us it has been a source of real joy – life means much more now that we see it from a world-embracing perspective. Let me end with a quote from a super children's book we have (*A Look at Prejudice and Understanding* by Rebecca Anders): 'Prejudice keeps people fenced in; understanding allows people to branch out and grow.'
1983

- We have three black children, two girls aged eight and six and a half, and a boy aged 18 months. We agree that black families are best for black children, but all children are children first and black/brown/white second, and all children, whatever their colour, want love, security and the support of a family. We make every effort to make our children proud of the fact that they are black; and we do not think that we were second best for them – there were no black families waiting to adopt our children, so that the alternative was possibly a lifetime in a children's home. Our son's natural parents, who are both black, saw photographs of us and our two girls, and they were quite happy that we were adopting him, even though we are white. In fact, when their social worker asked them what they thought about their son being brought up by white parents, his natural father grinned and quipped, 'Oh, I'm not racially prejudiced!' We do wonder when social workers talk of black families for black children what they intend for mixed-race children. If they too grow up in a black family, will they feel proud of their white heritage? The elder of our two daughters had a white mother and, if she had kept her, our daughter would have been brought up in a white family anyway.

1983

Jeff, Kirsty, Catriona, Rick and Fiona.

- We have two daughters of mixed parentage (nine and six years old, and Anglo-Caribbean), both of whom would have been brought up by white mothers if they had remained in their natural families. However, we think it is essential to acknowledge and emphasize their blackness in order to try and equip them for adult life. We feel this is helped by having the two of them – although not natural sisters, they identify strongly with each other largely on the basis of their colour. We are also lucky that we live in a multiracial area, and both girls attend a racially mixed primary school. They have friends of all races, and have the chance to mix naturally with their black friends and their families. Despite all this, they do still identify strongly with white people and see black families as different. Our elder daughter says she cannot imagine what it would be like to live in a black family. So we realize we must not get complacent. It is important that the children recognize and accept their identity as black by their teens in order to cope with the prejudice and hostility they will undoubtedly face at some time in their lives.

On the more general issue of the placement of mixed-parentage children, while I welcome the move towards recruiting more black families, I do not see this as necessarily the answer to the problem. A major problem for mixed-parentage children is their racial identity and wondering where they belong. It is too simplistic to say that because white society sees them as black they should always be placed with black families rather than white. If all other factors were equal, I think a mixed-race child would probably feel more comfortable in a black family (the child would be less noticeably different and would learn plenty about white culture at school and all around). However, there are often other factors which need to be taken into account – the child's previous family experience (often with a lone white mother), the need for the security of adoption, difficult behaviour problems and so on. We also need to give thought to the timescale of the child – although there are more black families coming forward, there are not enough to meet the need at present. How long can some children afford to wait, particularly as many are waiting in white institutions or foster homes?

I don't think the time has yet come when we can disregard or reject what a white family might have to offer, particularly those families with more than one adopted black child, living in multiracial areas. It is important that these families are not undermined but are helped and supported. It also seems crucial to remember that the most important purpose of placing children in substitute families is to meet their needs as children. These needs are many and cannot all necessarily be met – race is very important, but it is only one of the many needs which have to be taken into consideration in placement.

1983

- 'Middle-class women see all coloured boys as potential rapists,' said the social worker, not at all keen on our idea of adopting a mixed-race baby. What amazed us even more was the reluctance to mention the word 'colour', and the obvious embarrassment when the subject could no longer be avoided. (This was clearly evident in talking with both the health visitor and the social worker.) That was 15 years ago, and a lot of water has flowed under the social services bridge since then.

  As Dan grew up in a wholly white and essentially middle-class area, we anticipated signs of disapproval. Apart from some early anxiety in our parents, however, we met no adverse reactions. My adopted daughter, who was four years old when Dan arrived, had a close friend of her own age living in a nearby flat – but there were no youngsters of Dan's age at that time. He was, however, very popular with the older boys, who gave him rides on their bikes and other such delights. There were the occasional oblique references to his colour – 'You'll melt on your bike' (chocolate drop on a hot summer day). But we always talked freely about colour – we had told Dan from early on that we had chosen him because we especially liked brown babies. I think I can honestly say that none of us had any hang-ups about colour and, as far as we could tell, that went for Dan too. Our daughter, who had a healthy sisterly hate for Dan at times, would have probably defended him with her last breath if he had fallen foul of the National Front.

  It was during his second year at secondary school that we decided it was time to increase our family with two 14-year-old children, both black – a girl of Indian origin and a profoundly deaf Jamaican-Irish boy. As a spinoff, we hoped that an older brother, who was very keen on football, would give Dan companionship and support at home. It started off that way, but sadly the honeymoon period didn't last, and they both gradually lost interest in the one common passion they had shared, football. During the third year at school, Dan's behaviour deteriorated and he spent a spell at the offsite centre. He responded well to small-group teaching, settled down, and was regarded as very different from the usual child referred there. We asked if he could stay on – convinced that his behaviour would deteriorate once he returned to the mainstream classroom. But one term was all that was allowed. He went back to his class, and since then there has been a continuing history of periodic truanting, abusive behaviour, failed homework and so on. All these problems were and are mirrored in his behaviour at home. Many of these are normal adolescent behaviour, but there have been other more serious difficulties in which the police have been involved.

Our other son (now 17) fancies Princess Diana, whose pictures are pinned on his wall. He was in care for 14 years, and grew up in the kind of multiracial environment in which he still lives. When he came, he had very racialist feelings about Indians, which have fortunately been modified! Perhaps it is his Jamaican-Irish background which makes him very immediate and sometimes impatient at times – in spite of this, he has settled down well in his first job as an apprentice cutter in an upholstery firm. He spent nine months unemployed – a difficult time for him and us. His behaviour deteriorated to a point where we felt we couldn't cope with him any longer. It improved, however, when he realized he had pushed us to a point of asking social services to find him another home and, demanding and irritating though he can be, there are now no real problems. He has a wide circle of deaf friends, both black and white, and his current girlfriend is white.

As for our Indian daughter (also 17) she is staying on at school to do A levels and is seldom a source of trouble. We had a few unacceptably late nights (when in fact she came home in the very small hours of the morning) and she started smoking, which we naturally regret. Dan (now 15 years) has two girlfriends at the present time – one white and one black. His folk hero is Chinese (Bruce Lee), although both he and his brother tend to show a great interest in black footballers.

We live in a multiracial area and have a number of black friends and acquaintances. Attempts to interest our three black children in their West Indian culture has not met with much enthusiasm, since they are all firmly entrenched in the southeast London scene. To the extent that there has been rejection, it is we who have been rejected – as *hearing* parents of a *deaf* boy, and as *middle-class* parents of a boy who identifies with what he sees as *working-class* families, or as *middle-aged* parents of *teenage* kids! In other words, the problems do not seem to be the tensions between black and white, but because we are seen as hearing, middle-class and middle-aged! Talking with other parents, it is clear that any behaviour problems we have are those of any family with adolescent children – having black kids has probably not created any real problem at all. So, whilst we currently have very mixed feelings about having *children* on occasions, we have no regrets about having a mixed-race bunch!

1983

CHAPTER 13

Institutionalized children

As we have seen in other chapters, children who have spent most of their lives in children's homes will not have had the opportunity to form the close, loving relationships usually made in a family setting. 'Institutionalized' children may feel insecure and unloved and exhibit behavioural problems as a consequence. Prospective adopters of older children will be prepared beforehand to expect these difficulties, the testing and the regression to earlier stages of childhood. What some families might not be prepared for, as one writer describes in this chapter, are the 'little things' that make institutionalized children different from 'normal' ones. It is not just the sort of behaviour that is expected between members of a family that will be missing from the 'repertoire' of the child who has spent most of his life in care; he may also never have had the chance to engage in ordinary family activities — for instance, to go on a shopping trip, prepare and cook a meal, or bear the responsibility of looking after clothes or other possessions.

Although some children become accustomed to the anonymity of life in a children's home and find it painful to have a family spotlight on them, the general feeling of the families who have described their experiences for us in this chapter is that once their children were given the chance of sampling life in a family, they slowly began to relax and then to learn quickly, eager to catch up on all the life they had missed.

One important bonus for children who are able to leave a children's home in order to receive normal, loving parenting in a family setting is that they are much more likely in the future to become good parents themselves. Their adoptive parents can help them to break the trap that seems to ensnare children brought up in care, namely that without good models to copy, they may become poor parents to their own children.

Adoption: the inside story

- Two of our three children are adopted, Dan when he was almost three years old and Simon when he was just over eight. Since the age of five months Dan had lived in the same children's home, set in its own large grounds. To our amazement we found that he had never been in a large supermarket – he went berserk the first time I took him to one! Because he had always played in the grounds and there was a visiting playgroup organizer, he was unused to roads, and we had some hair-raising examples of how effectively local vehicles could brake before he learned any road sense. He went rigid the first time he saw one of our cats. There had been a dog at the home, but he had never seen a cat before and did not know what it was. The first day he went to join the other children in the road he sobbed bitterly when the game ended, because he could not understand why they did not come into our house to be fed and put to bed.

  In Simon's case the effects of institutionalization were more subtle. He had had an extremely unsettled pattern of care, but had spent almost two years prior to joining us in an excellent and loving small children's home which rarely had more than 14 children at any one time and occasionally fewer. We were prepared for his extreme possessiveness with his toys, yet it was still a surprise when each night he cleared everything he had played with that day away. We also noticed that he had some boxed toys which he had never opened although they were obviously not very recently given. He, in his turn, was amazed that if things were left out overnight they were still there in the morning; and when he was given a wrist-watch he proudly wore it for a day and then asked me to 'lock it in the office so it won't get broken.' Ownership puzzled him. He kept pointing at items and asking, 'Who does that belong to? Is it Dan's, mine, Nicola's?' He took a long time to accept that some items were for general use and were treated well by all.

  He had an appallingly limited vocabulary. Because of certain unpleasant episodes in his life he had learned to merge effectively into the background – life was safer if no-one noticed you. As a result he had 'switched off' and never asked questions. So he knew the word 'tree', but not that 'the thing pointing out of the side' was a branch. Most vegetables' names were vague and usually a variant on 'beans' – thus peas were 'green beans' and sweet corn was 'yellow beans'. He also recognized very few fruits when raw. Presumably they were usually cooked or tinned when he ate them. One of his teachers gave him a pencil as a reward for some work well done (he had been unable to read when he first joined us) and sensed his disappointment. When she sharpened it for him he beamed his thanks – never having seen a pencil without a point he had not recognized it.

One particularly harrassing day Simon asked why I didn't have some 'aunties' to help me, and he wanted to know what day the lemonade lorry would deliver our crates. He had never seen a couple asleep in bed, and it was months before he dared to enter our bedroom and even longer before he could join in family rough-and-tumble or climb in between us. He was obsessively tidy, even folding all his clothes into squares, so that my swiftest yardstick of his progress in adapting to us is to glance into his room late at night – floor strewn with toys and half-made models; clothes hanging from wherever they landed when he flung them off, and Simon hanging half in and half out of a bed littered with books and 'cuddlies', being gradually crowded out by our two Burmese cats blinking from under his bedcovers. For Simon, happiness is an untidy bedroom!

1982

- Two of our three adopted children had spent several years in children's homes before joining our family, and although very different children, both had similar signs of institutionalization. They had no conception of the pleasure that our other children have in giving presents to one another, no matter how inexpensive (or even home-made). We are constantly amazed that they show no embarrassment at not having saved pocket money or done without sweets in an effort to give token presents, but at the same time look forward with anticipation to receiving gifts on their own birthdays or at Christmas. One the few occasions that we have managed to encourage them to buy, wrap and give something to a brother or sister their own pleasure has been obvious.

One very sensitive area that took us a while to be aware of was the fact that, living in an institution, children never witness adults in disagreement with one another. House parents keep their arguments for behind closed doors in their own quarters, and even inter-staff flare-ups will happen in the office when the children are not present. We found that even the slightest quarrel that my husband and I had with one another caused tension and fear in these two children, while the other three saw no significance in them, knowing that even happily married couples can get cross or irritated with one another. Children who have not grown up in families must have very narrow and simplistic ideas of love and marriage, and feel their new security threatened if mother and father appear not to be in constant agreement. In some cases it must trigger off memories of natural parents fighting and being excessively aggressive, which is often the cause of children having come into care. Although once we were aware of this problem we were perhaps a little more careful over our occasional disagreements, we did feel the children should learn that they had no real bearing on our relationship, and that we all have a right to get cross or angry at times without it affecting our love for one another.

1982

- Our son spent four years in a children's home before coming to live with us. To begin with he panicked if we did not have dinner at 12 and tea at 5 pm. He was unable to wash or bath himself, having always had it done for him, and was amazed he could stay in the bath to play. He was unable to make the most minor decisions, as he'd always been told what to do, and when living with us he discovered that legs were for walking with, especially to and from school. Another shock was that he couldn't turn the TV on first thing in the morning and leave it on all day, but that he had to play with the various toys. The first time I took him to the supermarket to get a week's shopping he was amazed at the amount of food I bought and by the fact that I could pay for it – he was panic-stricken I wouldn't be able to.

    One of the hardest things for us to cope with was his inability to care about other people's feelings: he was so self-orientated and had no respect for adults. He was amazed that I gave my husband more dinner than him. He also couldn't believe that if he had a nightmare he could come and wake us up to be comforted rather than get told off. He'd been looked after mainly by women, so did not know how to relate to my husband and wouldn't let him touch him or sit next to him in case he should turn into a 'puff'. This also meant that he thought I was in charge here, and that my husband should ask my permission to do anything. Pity he had to learn differently about that!

1982

- Mandy was ten and Peter eight when they came to us. We had been told that children who had been in care were often somewhat behind their physical ages, both educationally and emotionally. This we found to be true, but the real surprises were the many 'little things' which Mandy and Peter had apparently never picked up. Maybe the biggest of these was their inability to play. We thought that all children knew how to play, but Mandy and Peter found it virtually impossible and still, even now, find it hard to sustain solo play for more than 15 minutes without adult assistance. Our first Christmas was also somewhat of an eye-opener. When we bought the Chrismas tree the children did not have any idea of how we decorated it. It was while the tree was being decorated that Peter asked, 'When are you going to lock the door?' We didn't know what he was talking about, but eventually we found out that at the children's home the Christmas tree and presents were locked away in a room until Christmas day afternoon, when the presents were opened and played with for a short while before tea and bed. The tree would be gone by the next day. Needless to say our tree stays a lot longer and presents are opened much earlier!

Other little things still happen, though much less often than before. Their lack of general knowledge still surprises us. Peter was most intrigued recently by knitting, and sat for some time watching the gradually lengthening garment. He apparently had seen people knitting but had no idea what they were doing. Both children had very little idea what the days of the week were, and could not say what or how many months there are in the year. To help them appreciate the need to learn to tell the time correctly, we now suggest they read the *Radio Times* first and check the time on the clock before turning on the TV. Knowing left from right was also a bit of a mystery to them. It doesn't help to explain that we hold our pencils in our right hands as Peter is right-handed and Mandy left-handed! Sayings such as 'raining cats and dogs' have been a source of some bewilderment to the children. In most families this type of saying comes up in conversation and we learn the meanings probably before we consider the actual words. We sometimes tease the children by discussing something of interest to them and using as many sayings and long words as we can fit in.

When we decided to adopt older children we assumed that all the problems would be large ones. However, our biggest surprises (not really problems) have been the little things, which have really shown us that, however good children's homes are, there is no substitute for a stable family environment for giving children the really basic knowledge of day-to-day living.

1982

- Neil came to us 18 months ago at the age of 12. Apart from one brief (but happy) fostering experience at the age of seven, which was immediately followed by an 18-month, somewhat disastrous return to his family, practically all his life has been spent in care. He has obviously found certain aspects of family life difficult. One of his biggest problems has been in realizing that in a family the same 'staff' are on duty 24 hours a day, seven days a week! This means that if we ask him to do something today we are still around tomorrow to call him to account for what has, or has not, happened; if he asks a question today he will get exactly the same answer if he asks the same question tomorrow, however much he may dislike it. All very trying if you are used to keeping your head down and manipulating the system to your advantage. Sadly, he seems to find the converse equally difficult to accept – that being around all the time means that we are aware of his hopes and fears and are interested in his joys and sorrows. It has taken him a long time to realize that we really do like to hear about the good things that have happened, not out of prying or idle curiosity but because if something has given him pleasure we are pleased for him, and sharing the experience makes us more part of one another.

Neil's total disregard for material possessions is one thing – but his inability to make relationships is even harder to bear with. For a long time our son, Tom, aged nine, was treated as no more than an animated toy. Friends and members of the wider family who happen around are often ignored completely unless they come directly within his orbit, and even then a reasonable reception is by no means guaranteed. Should anyone call to see him, they are quite likely to be kept hanging around for some time while Neil decides whether or not he will bother to stop what he is doing and speak to them. The lack of interest implied by such behaviour is not, I am sure, necessarily a true reading of his feelings. He genuinely does not seem to appreciate that others will form their opinions of his feelings towards them from the way he acts towards them, that it is no good knowing inside that he likes someone if he makes them feel as if he couldn't care less. We find it very difficult to get it across that it really is OK to let someone know you like them, are glad of their company. He is obviously aware that there is a problem since he will say sorrowfully, 'I talk to a lot of people but I don't seem to really get to know them.' The lesson that relationships are a two-way process and have to be worked at is a hard one if you meet it for the first time at 13.

At times we have the feeling that Neil has spent his entire life

Institutionalized children

living in a glass bubble, in the world but not of it. Ordinary everyday experiences seem to have passed him by, and at times his lack of maturity and lack of knowledge of how the world ticks at even the most basic level is frightening. There is no doubt, however, that he has made tremendous progress over the last 18 months. He admits to finding life very hard at times, and one senses that it was a whole lot easier when he could lie low, keep quiet and let life flow gently past him. The great saving grace is that, despite the difficulties and problems, he does seem to have a genuine positive desire to make sense of this strange new world he has entered. Together we are sure he can.

1982

- Sarah had been in and out of care from the age of two, and when we first met her at the age of five she had been in residential care for over two years. She was lucky, as she was in a small home. The staff were caring, and she was sometimes taken home by them at weekends. She was the youngest for some time and had to strive to keep up with older boys. She still prefers to play with boys, and is the only girl at school allowed to play football – she is accepted because she has the strongest kick in the school! Sarah is certainly very aggressive. One of our first trips with her was to a swimming baths with a whale to climb on. I had to intervene to prevent her drowning a boy who had dared to climb up beside her.

At our locals PPIAS meetings we often hear of children with tremendous appetites, and how even quite small children are never satisfied. Of course they've not been used to being asked what they'd like to eat or to having fruit left in a bowl or biscuits and drinks being kept in unlocked cupboards. Children in care aren't taught to look after their clothes or to make them last either. They don't know where they come from and the supply doesn't run out. Frequently in large institutions they don't even have their own clothes, but share them with other children of a similar age or size. One of the most frustrating things with Sarah was to have mending to do *every* night.

Another problem with children who have been in care is that they can be fairly indiscriminate about giving physical affection. Only last week an old lady, whom Sarah didn't know, stopped to talk to us while out shopping and was the recipient of a kiss.

The most serious problems we have had to deal with are lying and stealing. Sarah knows we can't accept these and she's trying hard. Lying is so much easier in some situations – but often it is difficult to see why she just didn't tell the truth, as discovery is inevitable.

When Sarah came to live with us she did not know any nursery rhymes and could only sound a few letters. She reads well now but has never learned her nursery rhymes – a lasting deprivation. There is a right time in every child's life for them to learn skills or acquire basic knowledge. If they miss it, it's very difficult, and sometimes impossible, to catch up.

To sum up, an institutionalized child can be aggressive and destructive, have tantrums, lie, steal, be behind academically and *always* hungry! However, if they had not possessed some spirit and the ability to fight for themselves, the system would have already destroyed them.

1982

CHAPTER 14

Adopted children at school

One of the wonderful things about bringing up children, whether they are adopted or born to you, is discovering, as they grow up, what talents they have. Caring parents, who praise their children's achievements and encourage them with the things they are not so good at, are providing the positive environment needed for those talents to develop.

What it may be difficult for parents who have adopted older children to do is to assess just what potential their children actually have. They may have under-achieved academically for years, lacking the motivation to try harder since they received so little interest or encouragement at home. Or they may have exhibited their feelings of anger and frustration by behaving in a disruptive way in the classroom. When they join their adoptive family it may be the first time that anyone has ever really taken a concentrated interest in what they can or cannot achieve. They will not change overnight. It will take time for them to respond to the newfound attention, to want to please, and to alter the way they behave. It is therefore essential that the adoptive parents prepare their child's new school for the possibility of uncooperative and unusual behaviour, that they explain his background and solicit the support and guidance of the teachers from the start. This is when some families will be lucky and find concerned, sympathetic staff, as we see in this chapter, and some so unlucky that they are forced to hammer hard at the professionals' doors before they receive the support they need and deserve.

Adoption: the inside story

- As with most things in life, the problems you prepare for aren't always the ones you have to face. We worried that our (mixed-race) children's teachers would probably all be white – no-one to identify with. In fact, Ben's very first teacher was of Australian aboriginal stock. The snag? She just wasn't a very good teacher! We nervously sent our children to the rough-and-tumble of the local primary school. They learnt to stand on their own feet, and acquired in the playground a sense of democracy and racial equality that goes right through them like the letters on Brighton rock. Lovely! The reverse side of this advantage was personified in Mr M, Emma's teacher, who, objecting (none of his business!) to her wearing trousers instead of skirts, added irritably, 'And another thing. I don't like the way she *looks* at me.' Total bafflement, until the family doctor asked whether ours were the only black *middle-class* children in that particular school. They were. Added to which, Mr M was a bit of an MCP – and Emma is one of nature's equalizers.

Ben's birthday party guests were always white; Emma always invited black *and* white. Was this because Ben was the only child of Indian, as distinct from West Indian, appearance at their primary school? Or simply because the kindred spirits in his class happened to be white? Maybe, years from now, he'll be able to tell us. We're aware that, at 15, he wriggles slightly under the gaze of the excellent Indian lady who is his form teacher. He could in appearance be her grandson, and she expects more of him, one senses, than of the (white) rest of the class. Not a bad thing? Ben's last year at primary school was punctuated by desperate fights. We still don't know how much they were the result of singularly offensive name-calling by one particularly unpleasant boy, how far by boredom with the last year of what, academically, was a bad school. He soon settled down at secondary level, in a small boys' comprehensive, and has been in trouble only once – for fighting a boy who pursued him to the bus stop with racial abuse.

We sent our daughter to a private secondary school. To our surprise, it is proportionately more racially mixed than the local state schools. Both kinds of school, alas (and I work in a state school), have usually no textbooks or materials representing mixed-race or black people as achievers in modern society. This is one area where parents can press hard for change; often the lack seems not even to have occurred to the teachers. At my own school, one of the saddest things is to overhear black children putting down mixed-race children, as they themselves are put down by some of the whites. Yet American research shows, hearteningly, that mixed-race children more often act as interracial bridges in a school than feel themselves to be outsiders. As a teacher, I know that school is influential, but home much more so. Like natural parents, you do your best and cross your fingers too. And our own children, at 15 and 13, seem to have come through the mill happy and well.

1981

- 'Melvin is undoubtedly a severely maladjusted child, who requires specialist help educationally.' This was the sort of quote contained in the diagnostic report which we nervously handed to the headmaster of our local village C of E school. We were more than hoping, we were praying that this experienced man would see beyond what was in this report. We wanted him to see that to send Melvin to another 'maladjusted' school, immediately making him different from his six new brothers and sisters, would do more harm than good. Of this we were convinced. There was silence as this depressing report was read. 'I will be willing to take him' (we breathed a sigh of relief). 'But should he prove to be disruptive, I will have to ask you to remove him.' We readily agreed. We were all taking a calculated risk, going against the advice of the 'specialists', but we were certain it would work.

So arrived that first day at school. Suddenly this previously aggressive, 'know-all' little boy of seven was clinging to his new brother, only a year older, trying not to look nervous. Melvin was not the only one who was new. His teacher was a young lady straight from college. We hoped she did not know that first morning that Melvin's headmistress at his first school had reported him as being 'a child that always demanded attention and affection by throwing things, slamming doors and shouting obscenities'! Melvin first of all took a very passive attitude; he decided to sleep! Head on desk he would happily slumber through all three Rs! The headmaster in his wisdom advised the teachers, 'Just leave him, don't demand, let him feel secure.' How important those first few months were, and how disastrous wrong handling would have been. To have demanded just one drawing from him at this stage could have ruined everything. But, as Melvin became more secure at both home and school, he decided too much sleep was boring. Slowly and surely he was encouraged to take part in class activities, until he found learning could be fun. The delight in finding those meaningless symbols on a page could become words, and that words lead to a treasure house of stories – a whole new world had opened before him. The odd behaviour problem was generally sorted out without a great deal of difficulty, due to good liaison between ourselves and the headmaster.

Melvin started this school in September 1978, when he was seven years five months old, not having had normal schooling for over two years. Now, two years further on, Melvin's headmaster describes himself as being 'very pleased' with Melvin educationally. He is reading to a good standard and is thought to be an intelligent boy. His behaviour is good on the whole, with the occasional relapse known in most nine-year-old boys. It was not surprising that Melvin did not settle into infants' school and was disruptive in behaviour, because it was at this very time that his foster placement of 18 months' standing was breaking down. Any child going through the same trauma of a family break-up would have reacted in the same way. Because Melvin was a child in care, he was labelled 'maladjusted', 'violent'. We knew that at some stage someone had got to be prepared to take a risk and shake those labels off for him.

1981

- When our two children started at their new school they were also new to us. It was an unpredictable time at best, and of course their teachers were put in the picture with the request that we should be told about any learning or behaviour problems *as they occurred*. The first shock came on open night, when we went to see my son's work – there was none to see. We were told that he was disruptive, frequently left the class, and would not work. His teacher thought that if we would do the work with him at home he might settle in class as he gained confidence. In our keenness to help we made our first mistake, and agreed to do school work at home. My son's next year at school was a disaster; by half-term what little work he had done was of a much poorer standard than we finally achieved at the end of the previous term. His teacher told us that she really felt she didn't know him at all, although she was pleased he was no longer disruptive. In actual fact he was becoming withdrawn, although still a happy child at home. As we were having severe problems at home at that time with our daughter, we asked for help from a child guidance unit, and were visited by a senior social worker from the unit, who felt the first thing to do was to have both children assessed by the school psychologist. We asked the school to arrange this. After three months I rang the headmaster about the assessment, and was told he had consulted his staff and they were in complete agreement: progress was being made and there was absolutely no need for any assessment or child guidance. In my daughter's case we had worked through her emotional problems at home and her school work was improving; we were led to believe the same was true of our son, so for a while we relaxed.

As time passed we noticed him becoming withdrawn at home and occasionally found him crying. Apparently his friends at school were calling him 'Thicky' – he had also been sent to the headmaster for stealing. I only learned of this because his sister was at the same school! Again I contacted the headmaster, and was still assured there was no cause for alarm, but that he would make my son's teacher aware of the attitude of the other children. However, a few weeks later my son came home in great distress saying he felt so ashamed and he 'wanted to be like the other boys'. I looked at his book. The ten words he had been told to learn were unintelligible; he could no longer even cope with copying; he was now nine. Once more I went to the headmaster, who expressed concern and said he would see that the teacher took action immediately; but at the end of that second year no visible action had been taken. When, in desperation, I showed his teacher the little but far superior work he had done the previous year, her response was, 'He prefers to chew a pencil than work – one doesn't like to push in *these cases*,' and, 'What can you expect from these sort of children, poor little things?' She had even given him a relatively good written report.

I showed the report, and his books past and present, to his social worker, who had them assessed unofficially; and the verdict was that something was seriously wrong either with the child or with the school. As soon as the new school year started, his social worker spent the morning at school and was told that my son was unteachable, impossible to get through to, and that 'even when shouted at' there was no response. When she suggested to the headmaster that the psychologist should be called in, he still wanted to wait for another year 'to see how things went'. She informed him that she was going to insist on action now, whereupon it was suggested that my son would be better off in a special school or even an ESN unit. My son was finally assessed. He is of average intelligence but was suffering from a lack of vocabulary (not surprising after five years out of seven in residential care) and, having been given a specific work programme, has had the ability to catch up and eventually become an average student. The psychologist was most disturbed that we had had to instigate her visit; in her opinion the school should have contacted her department a year or more before. She also felt that my being made a teacher at home was what was affecting my own relationship with my son.

Why did things go wrong when there were so many good intentions? With the benefit of hindsight, I think the teacher's attitude was wrong. I'm sure she felt nothing but sympathy and tried to be too understanding, not pushing him to work and allowing too much tolerance on the behaviour front than she would normally, when 'normal' is what is needed – and we all know how quickly children pick up on tolerance of this kind. When their teachers finally decide it is time to knuckle down, they see no reason to do so. After all, they have been getting away with it for so long. The teacher gets exasperated, and the child gets a reputation that will precede him all through his school life.

1981

- After adoption day, I went into the school secretary's office to alter our parental status on our son's records, and was dismayed to find the following parental categories on the education authority's printed form: 'Real', 'Step', 'Foster' or 'Other'. I objected to having our names entered in the 'Other' box, so the secretary compromised by adding 'Adopted' to the list – which slightly diminished the joy we had experience at the court the previous day. I feel we are 'real' even though 'adoptive' parents. It was absurdly hard to get the school to use his new adoptive surname, even though our child was desperate to do so. School books continued to be labelled with his old surname, even though we'd had the school records amended. On the first day back at school in September – five months after adoption – I pleasantly asked the deputy headmaster to ask his staff to make an effort to help us by calling our son by his new name, and was amazed when he replied that this might be difficult! Yet the term before a teacher had remarried one weekend and asked her class of six-year-olds to call her something different on the following Monday morning. I felt that if they could successfully manage this, then more effort could be made over our son's new name. We had to write a formal letter to his class teacher showing that we meant what we said, and that we needed more help than we'd received up till then. After that there was no problem, but it required firm insistence on our part rather than delicate hinting.

1981

Adopted children at school

- 'Draw a picture of your family' is a common request in infant schools. Luckily our daughter's teacher was aware of her adoptive status, and so showed no surprise when her effort included white parents, brother and sister, little black sister and herself (brown). Another exercise often set in schools is drawing a family tree. In this case she carefully drew in our family and then added a 'side shoot' to include her original mum and two halfsisters. Quite ingenious! It does seem important that, as well as preparing our children for questions from outside the family circle, we ensure that teachers are aware that adoptive/fostered children need sensitive acceptance of their perhaps rather unusual family set-ups.

1981

- Teresa came to us nearly four years ago aged four-and-a-half. We had two home-grown sons, Kaleel, then eight-and-a-half and Gavin, five-and-a-half. We lived on an estate with friendly neighbours, plenty of friends for the boys, and a school parents and children were proud of. Kaleel didn't make friends very easily, but nothing to lose sleep over. Gavin fitted in with everyone at home and school. We had been trying to adopt children when we were asked to foster Teresa. A home had to be found for her immediately, so we had no time to get to know her. She was with us inside two days. She had been lovingly brought up by her aunty Cathy and grandad but frequently taken away by her unmarried mother, Linda. Her life with Linda was a mixture of being loved when Linda was feeling motherly, pushed aside when some boyfriends were in residence, and left completely alone, sometimes for several days, when Linda felt the need to opt out of motherhood. It was on one of these occasions when Teresa was alone that she begged sweets from a social worker. She was taken into care, and sent to the foster home where her baby brother had been settled for six months. It was a disaster for foster family and Teresa. So she came to us, a pathetically undersized and underfed scrap who shook continuously. After bursts of incredible energy she would collapse anywhere and sleep for hours. Though she seemed to have normal sensations of pain at times, there were spells when she seemed to feel no pain. She would bang her head repetitively on the edge of the stone hearth, put her hands into water that would have made us yelp. Her eyes showed no emotion: the deadness of them was frightening.

  For a couple of weeks I kept her with me before trying her out on the neighbours' children. She was an instant success. We should have been delighted but we were thoroughly uneasy. Why should we be uneasy because she was so popular? We were about to find out. As Teresa's health improved so did her ability to hurt Gavin. While he was at school she was beginning to be quite a pleasure to have around and made great strides in all ways. As soon as Gavin was at home – hell. Gavin began to be aggressive, spent most of the day in tears and wouldn't go out to play. Neighbours began to hint about the nasty things Gavin was doing to poor little Teresa. We persuaded Gavin to go out to play and I watched. The knot of followers detached themselves from the Teresa nucleus and pushed and spat at Gavin. These were his former friends. A few days later, I had managed to persuade Teresa and Gavin to play outside together. They were crossing over to the group of Teresa worshippers when Teresa flung herself onto the road beside Gavin who was riding his bike. Doors opened, mothers rushed out and converged on a screaming Teresa. I couldn't hear what was said, but fingers pointed at Gavin, hands shoved at him, and furious mothers sent a bewildered Gavin back home. My instinctive reaction was to rush out and tell everyone that Teresa had engineered the whole thing, but I knew it was impossible to expect them to believe that she had actually thrown herself just near enough to his bike to make it look as if he had deliberately run her down. I told Gavin I knew exactly what was happening and that I would stop it, and now. I hauled Teresa in, whacked her hard and told her she was not going out to play again until I was quite sure she was not going to take Gavin's friends from him. I did explain the situation to the neighbours, but I must admit that even to my ears it did sound like an anti-Teresa, pro-Gavin campaign.

School started. The headmistress, Mrs McPhillips, was a gem. She had met Teresa early on in the saga and had summed her up very accurately. She assured me she would let Teresa get away with nothing which would hurt Gavin. She was also at pains to assure me she wouldn't victimize Teresa. What a relief after the usual attitude of side-taking – you had to be for Teresa and against Gavin or the other way round. No liking them both. The staff soon noticed that where there was trouble for Gavin there Teresa would usually be, just far enough out of range from the tormentors to be thought to be innocent.

In the New Year we moved from Cramlington. We had planned the move long before we met Teresa. We arrived at our idyllic smallholding so thrilled with our new way of life. It was a smallish village school and had a happy family atmosphere. We weren't even too uneasy when Gavin and Teresa were put not only in the same class but at the same desk. As the days passed Teresa became happier, and we were happy about the light that was sometimes showing in her eyes. Kaleel was resentful but wouldn't say why. Gavin was so upset he couldn't even cry. We were suspicious, so I saw Mr Roberts, the head, to find out what was wrong. I hadn't even spoken to him before I found out why: it was play time and Mr Roberts was in the yard. As he came forward to welcome me, Teresa shot across the yard and swung around his legs. He picked her up, hugging and crooning. Gavin, who had been reluctantly coming to meet me, saw this, scuffed his feet and looked sulky. Mr. Roberts was full of Teresa: what a delightful little soul – so friendly, so popular, so clever. Gavin was summed up very easily – 'so aggressive, won't cooperate'. All this said while being captivated by this doll of a blonde and not so much as a glance at Gavin. It was back to square one and maybe worse. I made enquiries through other children, and found that Gavin and Teresa were given the same work though Gavin is a year older than Teresa – Gavin is bright and Teresa lowish average. On the first day they had been given pictures to count. Teresa had counted her five balloons and written the number in the required space. What could only have happened was that Gavin couldn't believe the work could be that easy and had sat there looking for the catch. Teresa was held up as the model pupil and Gavin the useless lump. The child who had taught himself to read before he went to school had to read the same book as Teresa, who was only just beginning to read.

We were back to the gangs in the yard with Gavin pinned against the wall. Kaleel tried to defend him and came in for the same treatment. I stopped the ganging up by wading into the thick of the frays and tongue-lashing the lot of them with dire threats. I also hauled out Teresa and walloped her in front of her fans. I knew this wouldn't endear Kaleen or Gavin to the children, but they could at least see I was defending the boys, and the boys could see I was right behind them.

Gavin is now in Mr Roberts's class. His intelligence is being slightly more recognized, though he works below his ability because he has so little confidence. He has a close friend who acts as an ally. We worried that Teresa might not be happy with *Mrs* Roberts, who doesn't like little girls, particularly fussy, attention-seeking little girls, and in particular, Teresa. I hope I did this diplomatically – I made it clear I had not stood for victimization of Gavin and I wouldn't stand it for Teresa either. I'm not very popular at the school.

We aren't yet at the stage when we all feel relaxed about how we're coping; but when we adopted Teresa a year and a half ago we were all, even Gavin, delighted. After the adoption hearing, Teresa bought Gavin a birthday card. She had never thought of doing anything for anyone unless she had an ulterior motive. I went all weepy at her newfound sincere generosity. They play together well on the whole. Most of the squabbles are of the normal brother/sister type and easily dealt with or ignored. Occasionally we have spells of the old Teresa, but they stick out now. They were the norm not so long ago. Usually they get on together because they like each other, and not because of what I'll do to them if they don't. We had a tower of strength in our social worker in Cumbria. He pointed out that it was Teresa who had to bend totally and completely to our ways. I felt a bully sometimes, but I stuck to this theory and it worked.

1981

CHAPTER 15

Single parents

Until the adoption situation changed in the 1970s, a single parent was rarely considered suitable as an adopter: babies available for adoption were almost exclusively placed with married couples. As fewer babies became available and agencies began to focus their attention on the many thousands of older and handicapped children in need of parenting, prospective parents who were single found that they were much more likely to be considered favourably. It was perceived that they could give a child their undivided attention — there was no husband or wife making demands on them — and it is exactly this kind of caring which encourages handicapped youngsters, in particular, to flourish. This is not to say that agencies placing special-needs children with single parents leave them, after placement, to 'go it alone'. Being a single parent obviously has its problems. What do you do if you are ill? Who cares for your child if you are at work?. Most agencies placing children with single parents offer them post-placement support and guidance for a long time, as well as encouraging them to accept help offered by family and friends.

Single men, as well as women, are now accepted as adoptive parents, although they may find it more difficult than woman to convince social workers that they can parent a child successfully and that they have considered all the practical problems. One of the contributors to this chapter, Michael, describes how he was assessed and introduced to Harry, a Down's boy, whom he has now happily adopted.

There are more single parents generally in society today, largely as a result of divorce and the tendency of unmarried mothers to bring up their children alone. The important difference between single adopters and single parents such as divorcees is that the former have *chosen* to care for a child alone. They do not have to adjust to a life without a partner. They have no feeling of loss; on the contrary they have a very positive feeling of gain, of creating a family.

Adoption: the inside story

- I adopted my daughter when she was five years old. I had been fostering her since she was two weeks old. As I waited to go into court, a social worker from the local social services department made it clear to me that he did not think it was a very good idea. The three main areas the guardian ad litem discusses, i.e. the financial aspect, the possibility of ill health of the adopter, and emotional back-up and support, seem very drawn-out when you are longing to have the adoption order and get it all over with. Once you come out of court, having had the order granted, and it hits you that there is only you between your child and the world, the pre-court investigations seem more relevant, and the support of one's family so essential. Finance is a permanent problem, and also permanent is the dilemma of choosing between one's job or one's child – only three months after the adoption I was on supplementary benefit. Now that I am married, I can see more than ever the benefits of being a single-parent family, as a single parent's routine revolves round the children and their needs. Once married, one is inevitably influenced by one's husband's needs as the breadwinner.

  The one thing I didn't realize was the child's position in the event of my death. I assumed that my next of kin would be able, automatically, to become her guardians, and as that was my parents they would naturally be able legally to continue her care. I found out only recently that when a single parent dies (natural or adoptive), that child is an orphan and anyone (natural parents included) can apply to the court for guardianship. The solution to this is to appoint the people one wants to care for the child as testamentary guardians in one's will.

  My experiences as a single foster parent for the last 13 years and adoptive parent for the last five years have been mainly enjoyable. Being a nursery nurse has helped a lot, and 30 children later I would say to anyone interested in the welfare of children – if someone as ordinary as I could do it, why not you?

1978

- Kevin came to live with me two years ago, aged eight years, and with a severe hearing loss. I had wanted a much younger child, and preferably a girl, and when I was offered Kevin it was agreed I should foster him initially, to make sure things would work out. I felt very pressured to take Kevin, as he had been waiting so long for a home; and as he attended the school where I work, all my colleagues took if for granted that I would take him. As a teacher of the deaf I was keen to have a hearing-impaired child, and I feel his deafness has not presented too many complications; but I was not sufficiently prepared for the other difficulties we had to face.

A few days before Kevin's first visit his social worker casually informed me he was a chronic bedwetter! I found this to be a major problem and often became exasperated with him, as I felt he could have controlled himself sometimes. However, over the first year together we managed to overcome this habit – with a great deal of support from my own social worker, who was always ready to listen to my tales of woe.

Kevin had a reputation for being aggressive, and was constantly in trouble at school. Academically he had made little progress – he was unable to write his name, or count to ten, and he had a spoken vocabulary of about 12 words. He communicated through natural gestures with a few conventional signs. He rarely wore his hearing aids or glasses, and his lipreading was very poor. I did not work in the same part of the school as he attended, but I was often in his department although I tried to keep away from his class. I think there were definite advantages at first in our being at the same school, but there were also major disadvantages. In May of this year I took Kevin away from the school for the deaf, and he now attends a very small private hearing school. Before this move he was progressing very well with reading and writing and (with less enthusiasm) with arithmetic. He now communicates mainly through speech, but uses some signs when he gets stuck. When Kevin first came, he missed the company of the children's home, and he was really very unhappy. He used to tell me a long and involved story of how he was going to pack his case and go away, and I used to feel very hurt by this. I am sure if I had had a husband to discuss this with it would have been much easier, but instead I used to sit and brood over it alone. It was many months before Kevin showed me any affection, and almost daily he gave some sign of rejection. The other main area where I would now appreciate a husband's support is coping with Kevin's behaviour. Alone at home he is the most biddable, helpful and well behaved child one could ever hope for, but when we are with other people he delights in testing me. In general he is well behaved, but there are times when he will be deliberately defiant to see if I will discipline him in public – and he still has not accepted that I will and do! I have fairly high standards of behaviour, and I think at times Kevin finds them too high. I do know that when I am not around he often reverts to very immature behaviour.

My other main problems are practical. The greatest difficulty is of finding a babysitter willing to cope with a handicapped child, and of not being able to accept unexpected invitations as I cannot find a sitter. The married couples score here, as they can join a babysitting group, but this is practically impossible for a single parent. I think in the early months I missed not having somebody else to talk to and with whom to share the problems presented by Kevin. I do not have any family living near me, and so do not have advantages of an extended family life. I have had to rely on good friends for support and help, but I find it almost impossible to discuss emotional problems with them.

When one is lucky enough to be allowed to adopt as a single parent, I think one is prepared to face up to the many problems alone. We are unlike those parents who suddenly find themselves alone, in that we have chosen to be single parents and have probably come to terms with many problems before the child arrives. I know I count myself very lucky to have Kevin, and the advantages and happiness far outweigh the difficulties.

1978

Yvonne and Kevin.

Single parents

• Elizabeth and I met for the first time on a Thursday afternoon in October 1976, and the very next day she came to live with me. We were both thrown in at the deep end with a vengeance! We both had to make an enormous act of faith, and I think we were both determined to make a success of things. Elizabeth, aged 10, had to show courage and maturity to embark on a new life, with an unknown person, in a strange district.

She had spent all her life until the age of eight in a children's home, and had then been fostered by a married couple. This fostering had broken down owing to various emotional factors, but the responsible authorities did not think that a return to the children's home, even temporarily, was the right thing for her. I had met the social worker responsible at a PPIAS meeting, and she knew that I was genuinely keen to become an adoptive parent. My quest for a child had been long and difficult, and I had had many disappointments. Now I was trusted and given my opportunity, so I agreed to act at once, without any preliminary period of gradual introduction.

It was not hard to love Elizabeth. She has an engaging personality, and from the start was demonstratively affectionate. I found that I could respond easily. My main problem at first was physical exhaustion. I am a schoolmistress, with an exacting job, and also run the house and garden singlehanded. Moreover, I had lived alone for six years, and it took time to adjust to the constant demands of a child in the house. However, the tiredness passed, and we soon established a workable routine, much as two adult women sharing a house would do. So far we have both been blessed with excellent health, but I do sometimes worry about what would happen if either of us were ill. I made no definite contingency plans, but we have good friends, and I think help would be forthcoming if needed. Elizabeth, too, had a great deal of adjusting to do. Her life with me is considerably more austere and exacting than anything she had experienced in the past. Although in some ways I am easygoing, I do tend perhaps to be over-stern about school work. Before she came to me, Elizabeth had never been made to take this seriously; and the new routine of homework, plus piano lessons and practice, was a terrific shock to her! Now, to misquote Hilaire Belloc, 'she does her lessons (more or less) without extravagant distress'. We do have fun at weekends and in the holidays, and she is a perfect travelling companion.

She is popular at school and in the local Guide Company, and I encourage friendships as much as possible, to counteract any possible ill-effects that the close relationship with just one parent might have. She never mentions her lack of a father and I just do not know if this worries her at all, or whether or not she suffers at school because Mother is a 'Miss'. Hopefully she does not, as we have both been very open and talkative about our situation with the other residents in the village. The adoption order was made in March 1978, and I enjoy and appreciate my status as a legal parent. Elizabeth, on her part, took the change of status and surname with her usual cheerful unconcern – and soon began to call me 'mummie' instead of 'auntie'.

At times I do feel the weight of sole responsibility, especially when behaviour problems arise, which of course they sometimes do, and would like to be able to share these with another adult in the house. But, on the other hand, Elizabeth so far has seemed to thrive on the one-to-one relationship and to prefer the absence of the more complex emotional situations which arise in a larger family. Friends tell me, 'Your house is now a home', and this makes everything worthwhile.

1978

Jean Barton with Adam and Tanya. Tanya joined the family in 1984.

Single parents

- I had always wanted to adopt a child but thought that, as I was unmarried, I would be unable to; that was before I came into contact with Parents for Children. They are an adoption agency that specializes in placing handicapped or older children. Adam was five years old when I first met him. From the first moment I saw him I knew he was the child I wanted. Adam is an attractive boy who has lovely, curly auburn hair. He has big, bright eyes, and always has a ready smile. I soon learned that Adam was brain-damaged and blind. It was not known if he would ever talk or walk unaided. I had met him at an adoption party and spent all day with him. As soon as I saw him I had no interest in the other children, and would have taken him home with me right then if I had been able to!

I saw the social worker at Parents For Children, and was told I could start visiting Adam at the hospital unit where he lived. At first I was shy of the hospital staff. I felt they were watching me all the time. I would find a quiet corner and spend my time talking to Adam, getting him used to my voice. I would say to him, 'Mama is here, Adam.' It seemed so natural for me to say this. As he got to know me, Adam started to respond to the sound of my voice as soon as I entered the unit. I visited him every weekend for the next six months. It was a difficult time, as I had a full-time, demanding job. There were some members of the hospital staff who were not sure I could cope with the pressures of looking after a handicapped child. I had to convince them I was the right parent for Adam. I had a lot of help from Parents for Children in this matter.

The accommodation I had was unsuitable to take Adam to, so I set about finding us a home. I wrote to all the housing associations in London and eventually one of them offered me a flat. With very little furniture I moved into my new home to get it ready for Adam. Those first two weeks together were difficult for both of us. Adam had difficulty coping with this big change in his lifestyle. He slept all day and night, and would not eat or use the toilet. This was his way of shutting out a situation he could not cope with. I just had to wait for him to come out of it. After two weeks he was back to normal, eating and playing and using the toilet.

He was with me a month before he went to his new school. He settled in really well and seemed to enjoy every moment. This was another big change for him, and I was pleased that he coped so well. I, on the other hand, suddenly found myself with an empty day. No job, and Adam at school from 9 to 4. Soon the novelty of being at home all day wore off. I started to think how good it would be to be back at work. I missed the company of other adults. As soon as my telephone was installed I spent hours on it talking to anybody who would listen to me! I wanted to keep Adam off school, and this I did for a time, but was reprimanded by the headmistress. I realized how silly I was being, especially as Adam really enjoyed going to school. Gradually I got used to being at home and soon found plenty to do. I became involved with a local project for the mentally handicapped. I joined a mother's group that met every two weeks. This brought me into contact with other mothers of handicapped children. All this time my social worker from Parents for Children was visiting me and phoning regularly. If I had any problems she was quick to help sort them out.

Although I have accepted the limitations a handicapped child can bring, Adam's disability has in no way stopped us from enjoying life. I have taken him on a camping holiday, and this year we went to Spain. I do realize that as he gets older it will be more difficult to get out and about. I manage to get to church every week, and Adam enjoys this very much. He loves a car ride and going to the swimming baths, but he is equally happy at home listening to his records. Adam's music is very important to him, and I try to keep a regular supply of records coming into the home. He know what he wants. When I put a record on he will listen to the first few notes; then, if that is not the one he wants, he will show disapproval by shouting and hitting his head. Sometimes I can go through his whole record collection before finding one he wants!

Adam's progress has been slow but he has made several achievements. In his first year with me he started to move about by rolling over. I would throw smarties all over the floor to encourage him to move! Last year he started to crawl and this year he is feeding himself. The biggest problem I have is finding suitable babysitters, as not many people are willing to look after a handicapped child. I still get some strange looks from people when they find out I have adopted a handicapped child. I can never understand their amazement: it seemed to me a natural thing to do. I could not imagine my life without Adam now.

1983

- I am a single parent/adoptive father. I first got to know about my son from one of the daily national papers, as they did a centre page on children who had been in care for most, if not all, of their life. The paper went on to say that the agency Parents for Children was dealing with the children that the article was about. I went to see Parents for Children, and told them I was interested in adopting Harry. I got a lot of help in the preparation for the adoption from the social workers at the agency; they were very helpful.

After most of the paperwork and the inquiries about me were finished, I started to meet Harry to see if we got on with each other, and so that he could meet my family, my mother and married sister. Harry came to stay with me every weekend and some school holidays. We got on well with each other from the start, as we had a lot in common: he loved Elvis Presley, and football (he used to support Arsenal, but now it's Liverpool), and he wanted a dog, which I have.

Once Harry was adopted I added my surname to his and he found it easy to cope with. While the adoption procedure was taking place, Harry was of school age, so I had to find a special school for him to go to, as my son's handicap is Down's Syndrome. When I started the adoption I was working as a dispatch manager for a well known London west end store but, just nine days after the adoption was finalized (10 December 1980), I was unlucky enough to be made redundant; and because of the lack of services for my son in the borough where I live, I now stay at home with him and teach him things, like cooking. When I was working I received a lot of help from my family, especially my mother, who used to look after Harry until I came home from work and in the school holidays.

I feel sure that if my son should outlive me, my married sister, who is 16 years younger than me, would take Harry to live with her. I never regret that I adopted Harry; sometimes, though, I wish I had adopted him years before I did.

1984

CHAPTER 16

Contested cases

Once a family has had a long-awaited child placed with them, they have just cause for celebration. It is not difficult, therefore, to imagine how shocked and confused they must feel if, almost in the midst of their celebration, one or both of the natural parents withdraws their consent to the adoption. What course of action should they take in the best interests of the child? They are not likely to feel happy about handing him back to a couple who may not yet be in a position to parent him adequately; and to uproot him when he has just begun to settle into his new family would seem unnecessarily cruel. Yet the child is not legally theirs. If they want to keep him they will have to fight a contested adoption, with the possibility always in mind that the natural parents could win; indeed, if they have solved the problems which originally prevented them from keeping their child, it would be an injustice if he were not returned to them.

In these circumstances it is essential for prospective adopters to have expert advice. The families whose stories are featured in this chapter turned variously to PPIAS, to their adoption agency and its social workers, and eventually to a good solicitor. Apart from the emotional upheaval for themselves and the child, they had to consider the financial implications of fighting a contested adoption, the length of time it would take, as well as the stress involved in court appearances.

At a time when the emotions are so furiously engaged it must be almost impossible to think coherently. Yet it is critical that families try to keep calm, communicate clearly with their representatives and involve themselves as actively as they can in the preparation of their case.

Contested cases

- We were thrilled when Lucy, a five-month-old baby girl, was placed with us for adoption; we were assured that the natural mother was adamant that adoption was the only course open to her, and that she felt it was in the best interests of her child. Lucy settled extremely well with us, was a happy and easygoing baby; she related particularly well to our two sons, and we all found it very easy to love her. The natural mother showed some reluctance to sign her consent, which concerned us; but, much to our relief, she did sign it when Lucy had been with us for just over four months, and we immediately put everything else into action, had our medicals, lodged the papers with the court, obtained a date for the adoption hearing and prepared to wait for the great day.

  Five weeks after she had signed her consent to the adoption came the bombshell – the natural mother had changed her mind and wanted the baby back. As the papers had been lodged with the court, Lucy was a 'protected infant' and could not be removed from us without the court's consent, though we could have withdrawn our application to adopt, in which case she could have been taken straight away. We were thrown into utter turmoil – we knew how much we loved Lucy and wanted her to be our daughter, but above all we wanted whatever was best for her, and we could not be sure our own strong emotional involvement did not cloud the issue. We talked endlessly, both together and with many kind and supportive friends, and could only believe another sudden and drastic change, and loss of the family she by then had come to trust, must be detrimental to her. In the long run, we felt, if she was returned to her natural mother the situation could well break down: we believed the mother's own reasons for wanting adoption in the first place had been the right ones, and we could not bear the thought of Lucy perhaps subsequently going into care and possibly ending up an emotionally damaged child with no family at all. We felt we had no choice but to continue with our adoption application. This in itself was not an easy decision to make, as we hated the thought of denying another mother her own child, but we had to keep uppermost in our thoughts what was best for Lucy.

  I rang PPIAS to seek help, and was immediately advised to get in touch with the most experienced and sympathetic solicitor there was in the adoption field. It proved to be a very difficult legal case, and we shall always be indebted to our solicitor for her tremendous professional skill and general concern. Throughout we also had the complete support of our adoption society, and especially of our social worker, to whom we knew we could turn to at all times, and who gave us a great deal of her time, making special evening visits to help us through particular crisis points.

The natural mother re-signed her consent shortly before the adoption hearing, then dramatically withdrew it again actually in court. There was a month's adjournment. The adoption hearing took place in another court and before a new judge. There were four very lengthy court days spread over nearly two weeks; eventually came the phone call from the solicitor to say that the adoption order had been granted, dispensing with the mother's consent, and Lucy was legally our daughter. By then we were so emotionally shattered we found it hard to believe. Gradually, though, we began to relax. We received the adoption order and got the new birth certificate. We had some concern about the legal costs after a total of five days in court requiring representation by counsel. We know that our solicitor did everything in her power to keep the costs to us as low as possible, and the bill we received was just over £1000. This was just about all our savings at the time – we felt some relief that we were able to pay it, determined just to enjoy our new daughter to the full, and to try our best to build up our savings again.

Then came the next big blow – almost six weeks after the adoption order was granted came the notice of appeal by the natural mother. We were horrified – Lucy was our legally adopted daughter, yet again we were thrown into a state of anxiety and uncertainty as to whether she really was ours forever. During the next few months the strain of never knowing when the appeal would be heard was almost unbearable, and as the weeks and months went by we knew that if the appeal should go against us any consequent move for Lucy would be that much worse because of the length of time she had been with us. I felt I was almost constantly in tears, and it was a very confusing situation for our sons who just could not understand why Lucy should not be allowed to remain as their sister. We were also desperately worried about the legal costs, as we did not know how we could stand another, probably even larger bill. We applied for legal aid this time, but under the complex regulations covering legal aid we did not qualify (largely because of the capital we were deemed to have in the value of the house). It was surely nine very long months from when the appeal was lodged until eventually it was heard in the high court. The three appeal judges dismissed the appeal and confirmed the adoption order, and on our counsel's application the judges awarded us costs to be met out of public funds. We were told that the judges felt that the appeal should never have been brought, and that therefore we should not be financially liable.

Again the relief was overwhelming, but it took us some time to be able to accept that it was all over and that Lucy was really with us to stay. It was anticipated it might take about three months for the matter of costs to be sorted out. So we were again left in the position of having an outstanding debt and yet having no idea whatever what we might be required to pay. Obviously the most awful worry and anxiety was over by then, but it did remain a source of some considerable concern to us. Once the appeal had been heard and the legal aspects finalized, our adoption society offered to reimburse us for the original legal bill. They approached the children's department through whom Lucy had been placed, and they agreed to pay half. Unbelievably to us, the deliberations over the appeal costs took another whole year – we received the statement of account just two days before the first anniversary of the appeal hearing! The result was that the law society had agreed to pay a little over half the total costs, and we were required to pay well over £500. With no previous experience of the law, we were surprised that having been awarded 'costs' by the Court we could still find ourselves required to meet such a relatively high amount. Again our adoption society offered to reimburse us, so in the end we did not meet any of the legal costs ourselves at all.

It is difficult to know how we would have come through that dreadful year without the knowledge that so many people were backing us. Above all we were grateful to our adoption society for giving us full support all along, and for meeting the heavy financial commitments. But we are concerned that, in the present economic climate, adoption societies and children's departments may be less willing than ours to support adopters who become involved in legal disputes and perhaps incur legal fees.

1980

● Kim finally became ours on 30 January 1979, but not without many heartaches on the way. Everything appeared to be going well, and whilst the mother had not given her consent during the pre-adoption period, she had given no indication that she would actually refuse. In fact, we had been regularly assured by Kim's social worker that everything would be all right on the day. Hence it was a great shock to us to hear that the mother had refused to sign the consent form. Fortunately this side of the adoption had been discussed fully between ourselves and Birmingham social services. They were prepared, in view of Kim's history, to ask the Court to dispense with the mother's consent, on the grounds that she was unreasonably withholding her consent. Also, they were prepared to pay any legal costs incurred.

However, when faced with this bombshell, we were unsure about whom to turn to for good advice – whilst Birmingham social services were prepared to pay our legal costs, *we* had to engage our own solicitor. After much discussion with PPIAS, we were put in touch with a solicitor who understood adoption cases and was prepared to assist us. In the meantime, the statement of facts (on which our case rested) was served upon Kim's mother, but she made no reply to it. After several visits by the guardian ad litem, and at the last minute, the mother finally agreed to sign the consent form. In spite of this, and whilst our hopes were raised, our solicitor did agree to attend court. However, in the end this was not necessary, the order was made, and at last we could all relax and enjoy being a complete family in every way.

1980

- A few years ago we adopted our then ten-year-old foster child against her natural parents' wishes. One of the complications of a contested adoption is that it takes so much longer than a straightforward one. It took 15 months from the letter of application to the courts until the court hearing. Then there was an appeal in the high court in London, and so the whole process took nearly two years. We also found the meetings with solicitors, barristers and the guardian ad litem a strain, as no-one could assure us of a positive outcome.

At the court hearing we both felt surprisingly calm – probably due to the fact that it was an entirely new experience to us: we felt like actors in a play. We were very fortunate in that all went well for us, and the local judge did his best to ensure that our daughter should have a happy memory of her adoption (she had to see the judge in an anteroom at the first hearing); and so at last, on the great day, the whole family went down to the court to meet the judge, who wore his ceremonial robes especially for the occasion.

Seven years later her father still writes to her on every birthday and at Christmas – and we are glad that he should do so. However, although he asks her each time if he may meet her, so far she has been unwilling to do so. We feel that this is something only she can decide, but that one day, when she feels ready to do so, it could be helpful to them both.

1980

- It was at a party organized by PPIAS in London that we were first introduced to our new daughter, and made our decision to try and adopt her. We met her social worker, who was also present, and learned that she was in the care of a south London authority and lived in one of its community homes. It was clear to us from the start that eventual legal adoption was by no means certain, and that even if we were successful it would be a long and protracted business. Firstly, she was eight and had been in care practically all her life – as the result of a broken marriage – and, although her mother's attitude to adoption was agreeable, her father was adamantly against it. Secondly, there was the question of her position in our family. The pundits had advised that on no account would we be able to adopt 'one in the middle'. We had taken Malcolm at 18 months, and Hilda at nine months. At the time of adopting a third child, Malcolm was 11 and Hilda five, so to us a 'link' seemed logical. Thirdly, there had already been two failed attempts at boarding out with a view to adoption. Therefore the social workers responsible for her were at great pains to avoid any further disappointments for her, and this unfortunately created additional delay.

By the time we first met her, however, the local authority had assumed parental rights. This was due to the inability of her father to give even some faint hope that she would eventually return to him. We visited the home to see her, and to chat with the house parents and her social worker. Then began a series of visits by her to our home in the north east. At first she came for a weekend, then for a few days, then a holiday, until finally she came to live with us just before Christmas 1977. The social worker made the number of visits required, and those social workers more locally based did their bit too, during the period that followed. The mother gave her consent to the adoption – the father still would not. The trouble was, he wanted his daughter to be adopted, almost as much as she did herself, but he did not want to be instrumental in 'giving her away'. He suggested that the shame would be unbearable to his family, and in particular to his mother, in Jamaica, if they found out. We respected his feelings in this. The local authority however, decided to proceed without his consent, but there followed several months of inactivity which did no good to anyone (particularly to our daughter). We had to query strongly the lull in proceedings before things began to move again; but the adoption order was granted finally in the county court without her father's consent – he had written to say that he would agree with whatever the judge decided. This was in September 1979, so the whole process had taken well over two years.

1980

- Seven years ago we had placed with us a baby girl (eight days old) whose mother was not quite 18. Although the mother signed the consent papers when the baby was six weeks old, we were told that she had very mixed feelings about parting with the baby. The day before the adoption hearing was due to take place, we heard that the mother would contest the adoption, and in fact the hearing was adjourned. We then sought the help of a solicitor, who we knew was experienced in adoption matters, as we felt it would be very detrimental to our son (then aged four years and four months), to hand the baby back to her mother without the judge ordering us to do so.

  During the three-and-a-half months between the adjournment and the final court hearing, we had several meetings with our solicitor, a visit to an eminent paediatrician to do a medical report on the baby, and a visit to our barrister in chambers. In our worst moments, we made wild plans to hide with the baby somewhere in the country, but sense prevailed. When the court hearing took place, the baby was eight months old, and we felt we had seen her grow up from rather a sickly, screaming baby into a happy little girl.

  We had been told that the worst news we could hear would be that the baby's parents had married, and in fact they did so, three weeks before the court hearing in the local county court. We both had to go into the witness box and be cross-examined by the mother's barrister. The judge ordered us to hand the baby back to the mother, and after the mother had spent a whole day with me and our son to learn the baby's routine, the baby was handed back the following morning.

  As will be appreciated, the above contains facts and not emotional feelings. It was the most harrowing experience any of us, especially our little boy, has ever undergone. It was made worse by the fact that other people, however kind, did not understand the implications of this particular (and unusual) trauma, and we felt we received little emotional suport from anywhere.

There is a sequel: the secretary of the adoption society had mentioned our Christian names to the mother (which we understand is common practice), and the mother had also managed to discover which area we live in; then one of the social workers from our borough let slip our surname, which enabled the mother to trace our address from the electoral register. Our solicitor was so appalled by this that he advised an approach through our MP to the Ombudsman, and the local authority was ordered to repay half the legal costs of the case. This was a small consolation only, but we hoped it would prevent future bungles of the sort which occurred here.

CHAPTER 17

Disruption

As more and more older and emotionally handicapped children are placed for adoption, the risk of adoption disruptions becomes greater than it was during those years when 'adoption' was more or less synonymous with 'babies'. Previous chapters have revealed some of the problems involved in taking on an older child. In just a few cases (and it *is* only a few – the adoption disruption rate is low compared to that of fostering), these problems reach a stage where it is more beneficial to the child, as well as to the parents, for the adoption to end. It is a painful time, a time when it must feel almost impossible to salvage anything positive from the situation, a time when feelings of failure and guilt predominate, for the child as well as the adopters. Until recently, very little had been written about adoption disruptions, so that it was also a lonely time for families – one of our contributors writes that she did not realize that there were other families who had experienced anything similar.

A more open approach was initiated by Kay Donley, of the Spaulding for Children Agency in New York, who introduced the word 'disruption' instead of 'breakdown' as part of an attempt to put the emphasis on *learning* from the situation by analysing what had gone wrong, rather than stressing failure. Using this new approach social workers are more likely to be able to re-place the child successfully in another family where the dynamics are different; and the original family can be helped to regain confidence so that they too are able to try again, when they are ready, with another child. The disruption can be viewed as a change of route which can nevertheless be incorporated into the original plan of finding a suitable permanent new family for the child. In some ways an adoption disruption can be likened to the breakdown of a first marriage. The participants can learn from the mistakes of the first relationship and use this knowledge to build a successful partnership, given a second chance.

Disruption

- We first saw Leo in an autumn copy of a PPIAS Newsletter and felt he would fit into our family. He was then aged seven, and our own children were a boy aged three and a girl aged 18 months. He was described as a mixed-race child with a severe facial disfigurement, of normal intelligence, with no behaviour problems, and surprisingly intact emotionally. We had previously decided that we would not want a child with behaviour problems because this might have a bad effect on the younger children, but felt that we could cope with the difficulties associated with the disfigurement; so we contacted the adoption worker and were told that the agency was working with another couple.

A couple of months later we were contacted again and told that the previous introduction had failed in the early stages. We said we were still interested, and were invited to the adoption agency's offices where we learnt the full extent of the physical problems that Leo had. We were also given a detailed account of his life so far. We went away to think it over in the light of all the information. We spent three weeks of intense thought on the subject and decided to proceed. We went to Leo's home, a hospital, where we were able to see him having his tea, without him being aware of our interest in him. We had a long talk with his doctor, and also with his ward sister, who had known him most of his life and was the single most stable influence that he had.

Two weeks later we again visited the hospital and met Leo, who was shy at first. This was followed by several visits to our home over a five-week period. We all felt the strain of this lengthy and carefully regulated introduction, and we put a lot of his behaviour at this time down to the strain. During a ten-day visit he was successfully introduced to his school and to several local families. He then returned to the hospital for five days. We drove there to his farewell party, stayed overnight, and all returned home the next day, never even contemplating failure.

As expected, he was very homesick for the hospital at first, and presented the usual signs of insecurity – bed-wetting, truculence and nastiness to the younger children. It had been thought that I might be of little importance to him, owing to the fact that he had been surrounded by women all his life. John was considered to be the one who would receive the attention. The reverse occurred, perhaps because I had to give a lot of attention to the little ones, so that he saw them as rivals. As soon as John left the house Leo would start to act up. He continually baited the three-year-old and tried to get him into trouble, soiled himself and the bathroom, and was very sullen. This behaviour usually disappeared when John came home, and I found it quite hard to convey the problems to someone who didn't see them. In between days of problems would be a day of fairly good behaviour; but an expression of affection from me would immediately result in nastiness to the other children, or soiling of the bathroom.

At this stage we began to feel we would like to defer the adoption and have a fostering status for a while. We were very upset, as we had believed Leo's problem was his disfigurement, and that we had coped well in integrating him in our town, and in situations involving adverse comments, staring and even abuse. We had not bargained for continued problems in the home; we had expected bedwetting, but not self-induced vomiting or faeces smearing; we had expected jealousy, but not physical violence to the younger children, or pleasure in the pain of a kitten. We were told, 'You are seeing a side of Leo that no one has ever seen before.' We believed that this was true, and that, since it was 'testing out', it must have an end. However, we felt quite differently when I gathered from the ward sister, who telephoned me to commiserate, that under stress Leo had been known to hit the most defenceless children on the ward, and that the ward had also had problems with him in the lavatory. We were very angry and distressed. We felt that if we had known these things we would never have considered having him. We now wanted the placement to end. This was not an easy thing for us to decide: we were experiencing much pain and knew that the child was also suffering, although he gave no signs of it.

Even now, two-and-a-half years later, I recall this time with deep distress – I have never cried so much in my life. We were devastated with the guilt of disrupting this child's life again. I felt that the adoption agency held me personally to blame for the failure of the placement. We knew no-one who had had a similar experience, did not even think other placements ever did fail. Even friends who had supported us when he arrived were less than sympathetic when he left. We discovered later that his adoption agency were going through two other disruptions at the same time, so were under extreme stress themselves.

We learned so much from this experience, including many things about ourselves: we learned that we were not as flexible as we had thought we were. We discovered we had a strong marriage – a lesser one would have cracked under the strain. We learned that it is very hard on the eldest child in a family to have an older child brought in above him. Our three-and-a-half-year-old actually put this into words, saying, 'Leo is trying to take my place.' We do not feel that details of adverse behaviour were deliberately concealed from us, rather that the problems of the disfigurement were so obvious and prominent that they were emphasized as being most important when placing the child. We realise now that we were foolish and naive not to have expected behaviour problems from a child brought up in institutions.

1984

- Terry was four-and-a-half when we first met him, living in a big children's home in Birmingham with about 40 other under-fives. We had five children: four daughters born to us, then aged 13, 11 and nine (twins), and our adopted son, James, of Jamaican/English parentage, who was nearly three. Into this six-year age-gap we and the social worker hoped that Terry, who was also of mixed Caribbean/English origin, would happily fit. We visited him at the home three times, taking our children on the second two; he announced, 'I'm going to come and live with you for ever', and after one very fraught weekend stay he did indeed come about ten days later 'for good'.

That was 11 years ago, and the lapse of time and the pain which was for so long associated with remembering have blurred many of the memories of the 12 months which that 'for good' sadly became. My main recollection of the early months is one of exhaustion. For weeks Terry woke early and noisily, and during all his waking hours demanded constant attention. It was painful to see that he could never be happily absorbed in play, not even with sand or water; always his insecurity and anxiety showed as he looked over his shoulder to make sure someone was watching. There were tantrums and tears, of course, jealousies and competition, but he did none of the dramatic things we had heard of, like cutting up curtains or smearing walls with excrement – he didn't even wet the bed. Why was it, I still ask myself, that the whole family – with, curiously, the exception of James, about whose possible reaction we had initially been most concerned – became more and more upset as the weeks went by? I can only suppose that it was a real mismatch of personalities; but of course all the unspoken anger and resentment at what seemed the collapse of a previously loving and happy family life became focused on Terry. We knew that our eldest daughter particularly was suffering the misery of increasingly hostile feelings and the guilt that these feelings engendered, and there came a time at last when we grown-ups confessed to each other that we couldn't go on. At that moment we recognized, to our shame and horror, that what we felt for Terry, despite all our efforts and desperate prayers, was nearer hate than love. To write this even now is still deeply shaming, but it is the truth.

There seemed nothing for it then but to tell our (most sympathetic) social worker and for arrangements to be made for Terry to go back. It was nearly three more months before he did, during which we tried to prepare him and explain that 'they' were looking for a family for him where he would be happier than with us. The day he left, collected by two social workers he had never met before, he didn't look back as the car drove away. We don't know what became of him; although our own social worker visited him once in the assessment centre where he had been temporarily placed, our subsequent letters to his local authority asking for news of him were not answered.

What was to be learnt from this experience, destructive to us and no doubt even more deeply so to Terry? Looking back now, across the experience of a subsequent successful adoption (for some years later, plucking up courage to approach adoption agencies again, we discovered that they accepted our failure in a way that we could not ourselves, and were prepared to consider us once more), one important realization has to do with feelings – the feelings that we either did not recognize or did not give sufficient weight to, or that we suppressed because we did not want to recognize them, with fatal results. Because we so wanted to take into our family this 'older child', we refused to accept the strong advice against it given us by the experienced adoption officer who first interviewed us (and rejected our application) and the anxieties of grandparents. When we met Terry, red signals came thick and fast – the children's unwillingness to visit the home a second time, the tensions felt by the adults, the lack of preparation for Terry and ourselves, my mistakes and sense of panic during his trial weekend stay and (reddest signal of all, perhaps) our eldest daughter's anguished 'Do we *have* to have him?' Why didn't we heed them? Once he was with us there were many more, but by then it seemed too late to stop – until we eventually came to the final grinding halt. These mistakes were ours, we can blame no-one else for them; but might we have been helped to avoid disaster if the actual adoption procedures had been different? Although that is by now an unanswerable question, our more recent adoption experience suggests that we might.

One vital fact was different – Nathan, aged six and a half, was to be the youngest child in our family – but everything was done differently from the start as well. The supervisor of his children's home, this time a small 'family' one where Nathan, like Terry, had lived all his life, was 100 per cent behind the idea of adoption and was closely involved throughout, whereas Terry's matron seemed to have little part in the decision about his future and certainly saw very little of us. Nathan's social worker had known him for some time, and also knew his mother, his siblings and the home; Terry's had been assigned to him only a few weeks before our meeting. Nathan's past history, personality and problems were talked over with us at length before we ever had him to visit, but of Terry we learned almost nothing before he came to us. It was all a rush with Terry, but with Nathan there was no sense of hurry, no limit set on mutual visiting and so on, and we all had time to be surer.

Contrasts continued after Nathan moved in. His social worker and ours visited quite often; we were encouraged to remain in close contact with the home supervisor (telephone conversations with him in the first few weeks helped enormously with early doubts and problems, and Nathan spoke to him too when he wanted to); and, because we had met them, we could talk to Nathan about his old friends, his brother and sister, and his previous life. He received phone calls, birthday presents, Christmas cards. Nothing of this was possible for Terry; we could recall nothing of his past life for him, no-one from it spoke or wrote to him or to us once he had come – he, and we, completely cut off. We felt desperate, alone, and afraid to reveal our doubts and unhappiness; and what loneliness and bewilderment did *he* feel? With Nathan, we were helped and supported, and he was able, whatever inner anxieties and confusion he endured, to hold on to a continuity in his life. I am sure that this whole framework of support for both Nathan and ourselves enabled us all to 'take it as it came', not to try too hard, not to equate crisis with failure, and to wait for the love to grow.

1984

● We met Alan at an adoption party in March 1979. He was a small, backward 12-year-old – we assumed he was about eight or nine. In July we finally began introductions. In late August he came to live with us and stayed for two-and-a-half years. A few days after his 15th birthday, he went back into a children's home. Now, two years later still, aged 17, he is about to leave his second foster family (with their rather anxious blessing) to move into a council house with two teenage girls from his former Children's Home. O levels and CSEs under his belt, he is studying for two A levels and working part-time in the local market. We see him regularly. He is a well-built, smart, courteous young man. We love him dearly and feel privileged to know him.

This brief history does not reveal the anguish and despair we experienced during our time together. Our son had only been in care for nine months when we met him, but his early history is the oft-heard, sorry tale of frequent moves and lack of concerned caretakers. He had no concept of family life, other than the 'child-in-care's-eye-view' fed by the TV, etc., and no preparation whatsoever for his placement with us. Indeed, he insisted throughout his time with us that he had been placed for fostering without being consulted, and that he had no wish to become our son by adoption. We, being beginners, failed to recognize these danger signals and, despite our orginal wish for a younger child, continued to feel very committed to him on the basis of our strong mutual attraction at the adoption party.

Our own excellent social worker planned the introductions (and tried to encourage our son's social worker to undertake some preparation work with him). Just as Alan was to come to live with us, his social worker suddenly left ... and his new social worker decided to postpone the placement. However, seeing Alan's obvious bewilderment and distress, she relented, and determined to undertake a life-story book and other preparatory work once he was placed with us and felt settled. But her well-meant plans came to nothing. Alan resolutely refused to discuss his life and his feelings with her or with us, and rejected all efforts to help him keep up contact with his aunt, to make contact with his father, to trace his mother. Nor would he acknowledge that *he* had any part to play in making the placement work. *We* had chosen him – so *we* could make it work. Since he had no intention of allowing us to encroach on his life in any way, it was a relief to find that he was, on the whole, a socially adept, conforming boy, who was almost alarmingly keen to take on the manners, attitudes – and material trappings! – of a middle class way of life. We found we had many interests (and a sense of humour) in common, and we continued to feel a very strong attraction to him. For a year or so, though we got to know him only through the familiarity bred of day-to-day living, the placement held together.

But we still had strong needs as parents, the needs we had orginally had, to love, to nurture, to share our lives with a responsive child. Alan gave almost nothing of himself; and we could give only so much to a child who was determined to remain independent and self-contained. We made a number of attempts to add to our family, convinced that this would help us and Alan, but Alan would have none of it, and we and the social workers concerned dared not proceed. By the time we moved north, two years after Alan's arrival, we were feeling very much out of control. It was not so much that Alan's behaviour presented real problems as that we felt we were living with a withdrawn and hostile stranger. My husband and Alan, who had always got on easily and well together, could still talk civilly; but Alan and I found communication almost impossible. Was his fantasy, his ideal mother, his real mother he had never known, coming between us? Did he feel he was at last getting involved with us, and were such feelings threatening and unwelcome? Over the New Year holiday, Alan and I decorated his bedroom, a Herculean task. He found fault with everything I did, poured scorn on all I said. Other teenagers no doubt behave like this, but they and their parents have many years of shared love and care behind them. We had never felt close to Alan. His second social worker had left, and there was a gap of several months before a new social worker from our local social services was appointed. She was wise, sympathetic, concerned – but Alan would have none of her, other than to insist to us that he would speak to her about the problems that *we* (that is, my husband and I) were having, though he had nothing to say to her when they met.

His 15th birthday party was a disaster – cigarette burns, spilled drink, vomit.... We were angry but not unsympathetic, for he had obviously not been able to control events. But he refused to acknowledge any responsibility and, accusing us of persecuting him, decided to leave immediately. He left with one suitcase and we didn't see him again for nearly a year. After the relief at his going came the guilt – and the grief, as I packed up more than two years of his life to send after him. Shakily and slowly we began to rebuild our lives, to regain our basic optimism and self-confidence. Alan's social worker visited us several times to help us let go, and to give us news of him. Alan's social services department curtly washed its hands of us – and of him ... for he went into a local children's home, where he made life a misery for everyone for several months.

Then he reluctantly went to a meeting of the local in-care

group, and seems at last to have started to confront his past and his feelings. A large and cheerful family he had met through his judo classes offered to foster him, and, desperate to get out of the children's home, he agreed to go to live with them and to stick to the contract his social worker drew up. One evening he turned up on our doorstep; he was 'just passing' and had decided to drop in. The sociable, humorous Alan we remembered from so long ago was back, grown up now, and wiser and somehow freer. With his 'return' to us as a visiting son, we too feel free to open up our lives. We have recently been approved again as adopters, and are awaiting our new family. Perhaps we gave what we could to Alan, who took from us what he needed and could use. Other placements with other people supplied other needs in ways which we could not. Once we feared that Alan himself would repeat the sad story of his conception, birth and rejection. This fear is banished at last. Now we look forward to sharing in his enjoyment of college and career, and, in due course, to rejoicing in our new roles of honorary parents-in-law and honorary grandparents!

1984

- Our experience of disruption happened six years ago. I still ponder over how Davey is doing now. He was eight months old when he arrived. The preamble to the placement seems, in retrospect, to be of some importance. Our daughter was then two-and-a-half. We adopted her as a baby; we reapplied to the same agency when she was two, and were put on the waiting list without being vetted. We were told to expect a long wait. The association wrote seven months later, regretting that they were closing. We were advised to reapply to be assessed by our local borough. Their lists were closed. Just prior to closing, however, the association informed us that they had managed to find a baby (we had not pressurized or criticised them on the matter of their closing down) through BAAF. We were invited to go and see Davey, who was staying in a short-term foster home some 140 miles north of London. We were left with him for 15 minutes and then sent to have lunch to talk it over. Davey then returned with us. We had been given only the very briefest details about him but, as the placement of our daughter had taken similar lines, we were not too alarmed. Davey's foster mother mentioned, however, that he never slept. Our social worker remarked afterwards that Davey would sleep better were we not to overfeed him, causing him wind!

Davey was an advanced, handsome boy – more of a toddler than a baby. He was nearly walking unaided. He loved attention, and would demand this vociferously. He slept less than an adult's average seven to eight hours. He would doze off and wake up, trembling and breathing fast. He would scream constantly and not stop until taken into bed with us, where he would begin to play, relaxing as he was in close human proximity. If not attended to, he would scream for long periods, banging his head. I might have managed Davey on his own, but the effect on our daughter was disturbing. She changed from a chatty, relaxed extrovert, who was just enjoying her first month at playschool, to a clinging child who struggled to keep herself awake to fit in with Davey's exhausting hours. This tired her completely, and she cried incessantly. We contacted our social worker, who promised to come in three weeks, telling me it was a healthy sign that I vented my feeling by yelling at the children (and I did!). We asked the local social services for help. Their final diagnosis was that the situation would not change within the foreseeable future. We thus decided that Davey's placement with us was wrong for him, since he needed the attention of more adults and/or older siblings well beyong toddlerhood, and for our daughter, since the presence of this energetic boy encroached upon her to the extent that she could not compete with him, for us. We felt very guilty, but at the same time sure we had made the right decision. We would, however, have liked to have had some further news about Davey. We cared for him and felt it important to know that he settled in with the right family.

We spent two years being reassessed by our local authority. They turned us down since we had not lived long enough in our present house! We then approached a neighbouring borough and were approved. We are now being introduced to a five-year-old girl. Everyone concerned with her is helping tremendously. We are now going through a very caring, sensitive time, so different from the rushed, ill-prepared placement which went wrong.

1984

CHAPTER 18

Tales of the unexpected

This chapter, unlike the others in this book, does not focus on one particular aspect of adoption. Instead it brings together three quite different stories with one common element — the unexpected. For most of us life has a few surprises, twists and turns of fate, of both the pleasant and not so pleasant kind. Consider how most people in the western world meet their future partner. It is often by chance, probably unexpectedly, perhaps at a party. The first story in this chapter recalls just such an unexpected, chance encounter; but the characters are not those we have come to expect in a normal love story and the party is an adoption party. The unexpected element in the second tale is of a different kind, and concerns a family's 'solution' to the problem of their son's increasingly difficult behaviour — a solution which is a far cry from their original intentions. The final story is *full* of surprises — it simply has to be read to be believed.

Put together, the three accounts demonstrate the need for adopters to be adaptable people. It is unwise of prospective parents to have too rigid ideas about the type of child they would like to adopt or, once they have built their family, to have too rigid expectations of their children's development. Plans for the future may need to be flexible enough to encompass the unexpected.

Tales of the unexpected

● Adoption parties aren't for the faint-hearted. We have had a few ups and downs in many years of marriage, but going to one adoption party led directly to the most bitter disappointment we have experienced and another to the greatest imaginable joy.

Make no mistake about it: couples seeking children through parties (especially if, like us, they are childless and very desirous of having children) lay their innermost feelings on the line. And your feelings may be badly hurt, as ours were, by kind and well-meaning social workers who have to take hard decisions, like choosing between two suitable families. But there is joy if you fall in love with a child or children and it looks like turning into a permanent relationship.

Adoption parties aren't for anyone lacking stamina. I teach 32 children day by day in a primary school. I would reckon that the two hours at a party involves an outlay of physical and emotional energy equivalent to a week's work at school. You are trying, all at the same time, to talk to, entertain and observe children in a boisterous group who are complete strangers to you and to each other. At the end you feel tired and possibly baffled. But it is because the children are boisterous that adoption parties are OK. If they were not parties but sober meetings, the children could feel like cattle on parade at an auction ring. Because the party is fun, few of them feel like that for long.

It goes very quickly. Shy arrivals, games, some conversation of the 'And what do you like going at school?' variety at tea-time, then some poor soul trying to organize twenty very excited children for team games and sometimes succeeding. Before you know it, it is all over. Social workers arrive, ice creams, quick hellos and goodbyes. Then they've gone; and you will be left wondering who was who and what it might lead to and who the opposition might be (well, yes, I am afraid that if several couples are interested in one child, then the others become the 'opposition').

Admist all this feverish party-giving stand those rocks (or anchors), the super ladies who brought us all together in the first place and did so much of the organization. Perhaps not so much anchors as wise owls. They have seen it all before and watch with unblinking eyes (though there is something about each party that is different). If some child finds a home he so badly needs, it will all have been worthwhile.

But, dear prospective parent, this is only the beginning. The PPIAS parties are on a Sunday. On Monday morning comes the start of the phone calls, to social workers. If you're lucky they'll be in and can talk to you. One bit of advice: don't try to save money on phone calls by calling in the afternoon – the social worker is bound to be out. The phone calls may go on for days, weeks or even months. If you are interested in a child, don't give up until someone says a definite 'no'. Don't despair when the social worker goes on holiday for a couple of weeks. They deserve every day of leave they get, and usually take a slice of it in the middle of the phone-call period. If it gets a bit much, have a chat with an Owl – they are wise, have seen it all before, and are a great help. If you are lucky, the phone calls could turn into a visit by a social worker, which may mean that your hopes are being realized or that your cruellest disappointment is to come. He will ask the most gruelling questions, but then if you are an approved adopter you will know all about that. By this time you have virtually forgotten what the child looks like. Yet remember, you did fall in love – you have actually *met* the child, so different from the usual matching arranged entirely by social workers. So much better, so risky, so exhausting, such fun and so full of promise.

1982

- We have had James for four-and-a-half years. He's now fourteen-and-a-half. Patrick was born to us six-and-a-half years ago, and Daniel 28 months ago. We read the PPIAS Newsletter avidly, and must admit to increasing wistfulness that our son might settle down in our family as so many other adopted children appear to have done. During last year, our most difficult time yet, we began to wonder whether we could do any more for him. His behaviour, which was never very good, became even more extreme. He was constantly shoplifting, stealing from other boys and us, and coming home late from school practically every night because he had detentions after being sent out of classes. All in all, he demonstrated a complete lack of ability to cope in his first year at secondary school. The balloon went up when he attempted to run away twice within a month. We decided we would have to seek outside help. We had moved south from Scotland a year previously, so constant contact with our wonderful social worker there had ended. We phoned her and discussed the possibility of psychiatric help for him. Our family doctor proved most supportive and readily agreed to refer us. We felt we should try anything available.

    Although James had always been a problem, we kept hoping

we might be on the verge of a breakthrough. We believe that because of his ten years in a children's home his heart had become rock-hard, to enable him to cope with his emotional deprivation. Only by constant love, care and discipline could we ever break through the shell. Ironically, after he ran away the second time, it dawned on us that we had in fact cracked the shell. He was actually beginning to have real feelings which made him vulnerable, sensitive and miserable. He had run away in an attempt to escape from this painful situation.

The psychiatrist felt that James needed a tremendous amount of therapeutic help which we as parents couldn't give. That took a bit of accepting, but it was explained that precisely because of our love and emotional attachment we couldn't do it. He sees the psychiatrist weekly. Then, last summer, it was agreed that a school place should be sought elsewhere. We still can't really believe what ensued. A school for emotionally and socially disturbed children had recently opened just a few miles from our home. It seemed to be purpose-built for him and he started last September. After the first term we faced the most difficult decision: should we apply for a boarding place and have him home only at weekends? He desperately wanted this but, being very impressionable, anything new always seemed better to him. On the surface it appeared to be a somewhat retrograde step. Certainly it would transform our lives for the better, but that was not the object of the exercise! It was extremely difficult to put our own feelings to the back of our minds and think purely about James and, just as importantly, the younger two boys. Daniel was emerging as a very active and strong personality in his own right. However, Patrick, who was two when James first came to us, is very sensitive. He had been through all the crises over James. Although we had often sat down and explained that James hadn't had a mum and dad when he was tiny, we had the feeling that the constant upsets were affecting Patrick. We decided that James should board weekly. He has done so for a term and we are all enjoying the best time we have had so far. James is able to see us rather differently, and is finding school discipline very similar to home. We are able to recharge our batteries and actually look forward to seeing him on a Friday night.

It is turning out so differently from the way we had hoped and imagined. We are trying to reconcile ourselves to his never really conforming and settling down in a close family relationship; he has probably been too damaged by his ten years in an institution for that. However, we have so much to be thankful for – we are gaining an invaluable insight into the mind and emotions of our son. We have no regrets.

1983

- It's funny how life turns out. As an only child for years, not through my parents' choice, I can always remember wanting a baby brother or sister. When I was about 12 they adopted a little girl; but for most of my young life I wanted to be like my friends who had brothers and sisters to play with, fight with, argue with, share with. I grew up feeling that large families were to be envied.

  When I was 20 I got married for the first time. Babies did not appear, and it was seven years before my first child was born. When my son was three years old my husband and I split up and later divorced. I met my present husband, twice married and waiting for his own divorce. His wife had custody of their three children whom he now never got to see. My second son was born, and at that time the three children of my husband's previous marriage were taken into care. The first we knew of it was from a newspaper cutting. It took a lot of sorting out, and we had to be vetted just like any foster parents, but eventually the children were able to come to us, none of them remembering their father at all. What fun we had getting to know each other. Well, I'll pretend it was fun – it was hard work really – but the kids were great and really worked hard at helping to build our relationship. Our family then consisted of the baby Gideon, my son Matthew, aged six and the other three children, Philippa, aged five, Shereen, aged seven and Nigel, aged eight.

  Soon we decided as a family to apply to be foster parents, to try and make up in some way for the kindnesses given to our three before they could come to us. We duly applied and all went well. We thought, just short-term, over school-age, then I could cope. They told us that as we lived in a fairly rural area there weren't many babies or children needing short-term care. Then, lo and behold, a week later they needed a place just for three weeks for a 20-month-old little boy, Anthony. What could I say? He wasn't school-age, but it was just the three weeks (which included Christmas), so we decided to have a go. What fun that was, thrown in at the deep end, sink or swim! Well, it becomes a long story, but the three weeks have not yet ended, as he is now one of our adopted children and is ten-and-a-half years old! The following July his younger sister, Melanie, came to us, and they were both adopted together. We did have fun, Gideon 18

Tales of the unexpected

The Dann family, from left to right, back row: Keith, Pauline, Benjamin, Des, Shereen and Melanie; front row: Gideon, Mark, Matthew, Anthony and Phillippa (Nigel was abroad).

months old, Melanie 9 months old and Anthony just over 2 years old! I can't believe how I managed. Lie-ins were a thing of the past. I used to get up at 4.30 or 5 in the morning and do the living room out and the washing, so that when the children were getting up we could have some semblance of order. I had a super helpful husband, and right from the word go all our children had jobs they had to do.

Then we decided, after moving to a house with more room, that we'd like another baby. I couldn't have any more, so we thought of fostering or adopting a handicapped child. Our social worker was marvellous – she had to sell the idea to her supervisors, who thought we must be quite mad and even suggested a reassessment of our situation by another social worker, but luckily our social worker managed to convince them of our sanity. I only made one stipulation – any handicap but mental handicap. I couldn't cope with that! A little while later we had a phone call: 'We have a lovely baby boy, ten months old, fills all your requirements, needs a long-term home. Just one problem, he has Down's Syndrome – mentally handicapped!' She said to think it over for as long as I like. I spent the day crying and praying. Later, that evening, I talked to my husband. He said we could cope. The next day I visited the local ESN school and was luckily introduced to the mother of a toddler with Down's Syndrome, who gave me advice and books to read. Next morning I rang and said yes. For the next two weeks I went round in a haze of happy rushing, reading books and meeting handicapped children. Then I went to see Christian – that was it, this *was* the baby we were meant to have. He was living with some wonderful, short-term foster parents who had cared for him as their own. We still write to each other. Shortly afterwards baby Christian came. What joy he brought us all, how the children loved him, how we loved him, how our friends loved him, we all came to realize that handicapped kids are just ordinary people with special needs. He had lots of medical problems, though, and there were many traumatic moments. After he had been with us about a year he caught measles, and was dead within five days from the chest infection that went with it. We were at his side when he died. My husband carried his little coffin, and so may people were at his funeral, it was wonderful; he was the most loved little baby I knew.

We talked it over as a family, and all the children agreed we must have another. So we got in touch with the soical worker, and in August little James came to our family, only ten weeks old and very tiny. He too had chest problems, and despite all the care of our doctor and the hospital, after one bout of chest trouble, he suddenly died, just 11 months after we had lost Christian. It was like an action replay and almost unbelievable. My husband carried his tiny coffin and he was buried in the same grave as little Christian.

Just a few weeks later we moved. We decided again we wanted another child, but the social worker insisted we should not have another Down's child; she said it would affect us badly psychologically. It was rot, but there you are. So we moved, and on 'Nationwide' I saw a programme about the *Be My Parent* book. I went to see one, and made inquiries about ten children, including a 14-year-old Down's boy who was desperate for a home. The outcome was that we were contacted about him from Wales at the same time that the local social services approached us to have a little boy of eight, Mark, orphaned and retarded. We went to Wales and met Keith. We decided we could cope with both children, so both sets of social services got together, both desperate. Keith came to live with us first and settled quickly; then, as Mark desperately wanted to come, he was able to do so two months later. By Christmas (three months later still) none of us could remember being any other way.

By then I had been working on my social worker about a *baby*!

She was a super person; she knew we *all* needed another baby, and that the gap was still there from Christian and James; so we again looked round, and we found Benjamin – he came to us in March last year, aged 13 months. Only when we had Ben did we realize how frail and sickly our other little boys had been. Ben is fighting fit, hale and hearty, and really doing well; his antics could fill a book, and it's only since he arrived that I realize I *am* 42 years old. He is so bright and crafty that if he wasn't handicapped I don't think I would win; he runs rings round me!! But oh, how we love him. Losing Christian and James makes us appreciate Ben much more; the children adore him. On 18 March this year Keith, Mark and Benjy were adopted.

We now stand as follows: Nigel 17½, Shereen 16½, Keith 16½, Matthew 15, Phillipa 14, Anthony 10½, Mark 10, Gideon 9¾, Melanie almost 9 years old and Benjamin 2½ years old, not forgetting Des and me, two very old 42-year-olds! We have had many problems, many crises, many failures, we are not superhuman; we have sometimes been failures as parents, but we feel that most of the time it is on the plus side, and we have ten wonderful children, a credit to us and themselves.

1983

CHAPTER 19

The last word: the comments of adoptees

Children in 'ordinary' families must sometimes feel rather powerless, as adults seem to decide the path of their early lives. Children adopted as babies probably all have fantasies about how different their lives might have been if social workers had matched them up with a different set of adoptive parents. Children adopted or fostered when they are older take an active part nowadays in the decision-making about their new families, but they too must sometimes feel that the adults are still very much in control. The following comments from the booklet *Whose Child*, published in 1979, give some idea of the thoughts of children in care on this subject: 'There are so many people discussing your future and disagreeing, you don't know where to go — there are so many people, I'm lost.' 'They plan your life for you.' Much better plans than no plans, and the adults concerned do have the children's best interests in mind; but just what *is* it like at the receiving end?

So far, apart from chapter 11 ('Tracing'), this book has concentrated on the experiences of adoptive parents. In order to redress the balance, albeit very slightly, in this chapter the adoptees have the last word. They tell us what it is like for a child to change families frequently, and how it feels to be a teenager about to be fostered by a family for the first time. We learn what drives a child to test her new family, and what it is like to have parents whose racial origins are different from one's own. Of course each experience is unique, but running through all the accounts, despite the difficult periods described, is the very positive feeling which the writers have about their adoptive/foster families, and the happiness, security and love they have enjoyed with them.

The last word: the comments of adoptees

- When I first came to this family I was very frightened, because I had been moved from different homes before; they had been horrid. So I thought that, because the other homes were not very nice to me, this family was going to be horrid. The first night I came I was not used to so many people around the house, and I was very confused, but soon, after about four weeks, I got used to my surroundings. Sometimes when social workers came I ran away into my bedroom, because I thought that each time I would be taken away. I had used to always think about the past. But my foster parents taught me to look into the future, and what I would do and not what I had done.

  I wanted to be adopted when I found out that the girl who is now my sister got adopted, and when I understood what it meant. I did so want to be a part of a family and stay for good. I began to get very ill because I wanted to be adopted. When I was adopted I cried with happiness. Now I feel safe. I can now stay with my family for as long as I please and that will be for as long as I live. I love my family very much.

  1982   (*Carol, aged 10*)

- I am ten years old, and I have been living with a white mum and dad for seven-and-a-half years. I was born in London. Sometimes people call me names at school but I ignore them. I have a brother of 11 and a sister of 14. Sometimes they call me names but I say names back to them. We have just moved up to Scotland. It is very nice up here and we have a very good view. It is not strange living with a white family or being in a white school; it is just that I'm black and they are white. It's a bit funny to start off with. I have got a black friend. I met him in Cyprus.

  1982   (*Martin, aged 10*)

- When I came here I felt happy that I'd be leaving the home and having some parents; I felt strange when I saw my new home, but I settled down quite quickly and I was very happy here. The thing I like about living here is because they let me put up Madness posters on the wall and they let me have boyfriends and they let me go out late. The only time I come in early is school days, but every other time I come in late-ish. [10 o'clock is late to Amanda]

  1982   (*Amanda, aged 15*)

- I have been fostered for four years now. So many things have happened since I first arrived in Orkney. I was very quiet. I didn't have opinions of my own; if I did I never said so, thinking that it didn't matter what I thought anyway. Being in a children's home for nine years I thought it was my home. It was very hard leaving my friends and all the people I had known for years. I think leaving the children's home was one of the hardest things I've done. After all, I didn't have any idea what being in a family was, it didn't mean anything to me. I remember my social worker asking me what kind of a family I would like. There's no real answer to that question; after all, if you've never been in a family before, how would you know?

When I went to my foster parents' home I must admit I was excited. It was my first ride on a plane. For the first time I was leaving Strathclyde. I had been with a fostering family before that but it didn't work out, as I was the only child and so I was getting a lot of attention. This made me even more quiet, as I wasn't used to it. The Orkneys was really a big change. I was supposed to be staying for just three weeks. But it's nearly four years. We are a big family with three girls and four boys. I wish we had more brothers and sisters. I think the more the merrier.

I'm glad I am fostered, I've never thought it was different from adoption. I wouldn't feel any different if I was adopted. I'm sure there's some children who worry about leaving their friends and the place they knew so well. I've done it and I am sure anyone can. Your brothers, sisters and parents are the best friends around. Now I have a mind of my own, I know that what I think is just as important as anybody else's opinions. I wouldn't like to think what I would be like now if I was still in a children's home. I did like the children's home but it's only the good things I like to remember.

1983   (*Bernadette, aged 15*)

- After living in a children's home for 11 years, to live in a family surrounded by their things going on was frightening indeed. You wonder whether it will turn out all right. To be fostered at 16 was difficult, but better than living in a girls' hostel, where I might have gone. I knew my foster parents before I went to live with them, which was good. But for a start I never had a man walk around the house in a nightshirt before, so that was embarrassing. It was unnerving at first for both of us. Then the food was difficult to get used to as well; the children's home food was plain and here it was different. I must admit that it is good fun – you have your ups and downs as in all families. But they are a good family and I am enjoying myself indeed.

1979

- In a children's home, when you leave school you are unemployed, and you keep going for jobs and it gets monotonous after a while; and you start thinking you are not going to get a job and you just sit down in your chair, don't move, just watch television and feel sorry for yourself. Now my foster mother boosts me up, she sometimes tells me off, sometimes hurts me in a sort of way, but she gets me up off that chair and gets me to look for a job, and that's the one thing I think is important for us to have, to have someone to boost your morale. People who want to foster you, love you and want to look after you and want to see you have a good future. I am more outspoken now. I speak out what I feel. I am more confident in myself, going for a job now I feel I can get something and that I can go somewhere. I have got that back-up to help me so I think I have changed in lots of ways.

1979 (*Two fostered teenagers*)

- I was taken into care at six months, and spent the next eight years in and out of various children's homes and foster homes – eight changes in all. I went to live with my adoptive parents at eight-and-a-half years and was finally adopted at nine-and-a-half years.

  The day I arrrived at the home of my adoptive parents they gave me a doll. That was the first thing I had ever been given and allowed to keep – the only thing in the world that I owned. I could not believe it was really mine, but after nearly 30 years I still have that doll. I had come from having nothing and nobody, to having everything (or so it seemed) and *somebody*. My adoptive parents were childless and to me that was terribly important. The last foster home I had been in hadn't worked because there had been a girl only a year older than myself already there. I was jealous of her and she of me. I had had enough of competition in the children's home.

  One of the other reasons that I had not settled anywhere else was that I had been given absolutely *no* preparation beforehand – just picked up and moved, like a piece of furniture. This is a guarantee of failure. For this last move I had had at least some warning and been asked if I wanted to go. That was important. *Never assume* a child wants to move from where he or she is – always give the child the freedom to choose.

Despite the preparation, the final change to the adoptive home was traumatic. I felt dreadfully insecure – I just could not believe that anyone could possibly want me, or would keep me once they knew what I was like. I had awful nightmares every night, and had to have the light on all night for several years. (I'm still afraid of the dark!) I *knew* they wouldn't keep me, and so I tried every trick in the book – to test them and make them reject me. I wanted to reject them before they could do it to me. I fought, I kicked, I bit, I lied, I cheated. There was so much anger inside me that it used to erupt, every now and again, into volcanic temper tantrums. Then I would be absolutely terrified that they would send me back to the home. In between the periods of antisocial behaviour, I worked very hard to become sociable and do what my parents wanted me to do. Gradually the outbursts were less frequent and I fought less, but it took years rather than months. I desperately wanted the love of my 'parents', but could not trust myself or them enough to accept it.

Once, when I was ten, my mother was out when I came home from school, and I was totally convinced that she had finally had enough of me and left me. That was the only time for many years that I really cried (I had learned not to cry in the children's home). When she did arrive home I was sick. I was at my worst when, every month, the social worker came to see if I was settling in. I used to feel really threatened, and quite expected her to take me away with her. I would be literally dragged down from my bedroom to meet her, and then sit and glare at her without saying a word. (It was no real wonder she eventually pronounced me 'unadoptable'. Thank God the magistrates at Willesden disagreed with her and sanctioned my adoption order.) The first school I attended, after moving into my new home, was hell. I was considered to be ESN because I was totally illiterate and innumerate. I ended up being bottom of the bottom stream and consequently teased by my peers. Because of this I never played with, or made friends with, anyone for the two-and-a-half years I was there. With the help of a private tutor, and tremendous help and support from my mother, I did manage to pass the 11 plus examination, and once I went to the grammar school I was much more settled and relaxed. I felt 'normal', and more equal with my peer group. When you are living in care you feel like the dregs at the bottom of the barrel – not fit to mix with the rest of society.

Once my adoption was made legal I began to feel more secure, although still inferior. I think that one reason for my inferiority complex was that I had no information about myself, apart from what I could remember. I sometimes used to feel that I had just materialized at the age of eight, and that everything before was just a figment of my imagination! Sounds crazy, I know, but when you have no knowledge of your background at all, what proof do you have that you exist?

Having told you how I felt, could I now presume to give some words of advice to parents adopting an older child?

Please just accept them as they are – and not as you would want them to be.

Give lots and lots of love and security when it is needed, night or day, even if it interrupts what you are doing. Routine is a great help.

Don't ever threaten to sent your child away – neither in jest or temper.

Be firm, but be there.

Finally, may I just say that my mother reckons it was worth it!

1983   (*Christine Steer, now happily married
with two children, aged 15 and 12*)

- I was born at St Mary's hospital in Paddington. I was then moved to a children's home in Lewisham, where I stayed for about four years. I knew absolutely nothing about my natural parents, not even their name. I am not white and not black. I remember very little of the children's home, but I am sure that it was not a very happy experience. I always remember being told off by one particular person, a very large white woman. If I can still remember her now, she must have had some effect on me. I can't remember anything about the other children, how many there were. I slept in a dormitory with probably five other children.

  When a certain Mr and Mrs Walker and family came to visit me, I had no idea who they were or why they were so interested in me, but I do remember looking forward to seeing them more and more each time. I had party on my fourth birthday. They brought me a red football. It was then time for me to move, which I can't remember, but I had something on that day that I didn't have the day before: a family – a father, a mother, two brothers and a sister – and they spoiled me with affection, something I did not know about. I was cuddled regularly by my mother, had my very own bedroom with Rupert Bear curtains, and my very own teddy bear. Looking back on my life at home, I found it one hundred per cent better than being in a children's home. I felt loved and cared for. I felt part of something even though I couldn't work out what. In a home there is not enough time and care and affection for the children. There are two things that I still love to this day: to be cuddled, and to be loved, neither of which I had at all at the children's home. I then started infant school, where I made a lot of friends. I kept these friends right through primary school and junior school. I had a home to go to every night. Noone knew I was adopted until I told them. I wish I hadn't, as some of the children would be nasty. I couldn't work out why it mattered. My brothers and sisters were still very close, and we did everything together. As they were older than me I did get picked on a bit and called the baby of the family, but I didn't mind, at least I had a family.

I then went to a senior school, only for one year, before I was moved to a boarding school. It was at the first school that I started to be called names like 'wog', 'Paki', 'darky'. I wasn't that dark, but I couldn't work out why I was called the same names as negroes and Indians. As far as I was concerned, I had been born in England and that made me British.

When I left school and moved back home I was still loved and very much cared for. It was then that I started to rebel. I couldn't be told what to do by my parents, and the more they tried to help me the more I hated it. At 18 years old I left home, not really knowing what I was doing, but I felt independent. I had a very good group of friends who used to ask, 'How come you're so dark?' My reply normally was, 'I don't know and I don't really care.' I lost no friends because of my colour. All my girlfriends happened to be English. I never really came across any colour prejudice at all, as the people who knew me liked me for what I was, what my character said, not my colour. It was only a year or so ago that I got off my high horse and started to respect my parents again, and I do to this day. Now I am 29, and I still see my parents regularly: I still love them very much. I cannot express how much they have done for me. They gave me everything a lonely child needs, and they didn't waver, even though sometimes it must have been very hard for them. I will do everything for them – and I mean everything. My brothers and sister did very well at school and went on to further education at university. I was not so lucky. I left school at 16, and joined the Gas Board as an apprentice. Even though my brothers and sister were cleverer, it didn't disturb me, it did the opposite. I decided that I could, and would, do as well as them, but in my own field. Now I have a good trade and my own decorating business, and class myself as a first-class decorator. I was not happy to be just OK: I wanted to push myself so that I can be proud of it, and if I am proud, what do you think my family must think? I am happy that I have done my best because I can see the joy in my parents' faces when I tell them of my news. Not everything has run smoothly for me, but all I have to do is think about what would have happened if I had stayed in a children's home. The thought scares me. The best institution in the world is that of the family; the worst, I think, is a children's home.

Recently, I was told that non-white children are being sentenced to life in an institution rather than being adopted by white families. I couldn't believe it! If parents who want to adopt a child fully understand their undertaking and truly have love to give to a lonely child, then it doesn't matter what colour or race they are. They are still children, who only want to love someone and to be loved. My parents adopted me, I was not white, they were, but that did not make the slightest bit of difference. If people still have the misfortune to be prejudiced towards any colour, then they should not be in a position to tell others of their thoughts. We should all judge people on their character. This tells you more of anyone than just the colour of his skin. I shall fight against any kind of colour prejudice for the rest of my life.

1984   (*Kim, aged 29*)

I was born, the second of twin girls, in 1965 on a small island in the Indian Ocean, into a Chinese family who already had 11 children. My family was typical of many families on the island at that time: several of the younger children were constantly ill, and there was never enough money to make ends meet. My mother, who had been unwell for a long time and in hospital, was all the weaker for giving birth to my sister and me. She now had 13 children to look after. My father had a small grocery 'shop', although in European terms it was more of a roadside stall with a roof. So this was my family: but a family with whom I lived for only nine months. Then came my adoption.

In 1964 my adoptive parents (my father is Australian, my mother English) moved to the island because of my father's work. They did not have children. It was while they were living on the island that they decided that they would like to adopt a baby, if possible a Chinese one. Friends of my parents, an English woman married to a Chinese surgeon, knew my first family and of the problems they were having, and that is how the contact was made. My parents were taken to visit my first family to discuss a possible adoption. The visit was also an opportunity for my first family (and a lot of them were there, so I'm told!) to see whether they considered my adoptive parents were suitable. My adoptive parents also saw me. As a result of this meeting, my first family came to the conclusion that, apart from their love for both babies, it would benefit everyone to have a baby adopted. They were satisfied that my adoptive parents could give the baby a happy, secure home. They welcomed the opportunity of giving one of their children a better chance in life, better than many of its brothers and sisters would have. It was also assured of a good edcuation, which most Chinese consider very important. They decided that I, the second-born of the twins, should be adopted. I lived for a further four years on the island with my new parents. The year before we left we adopted another Chinese baby, this time from a different family. She was only three days old when she came to us. Our family was complete.

In 1970 my father's work moved us to India. I started school at the British school in New Delhi, and quickly settled in along with pupils from all over the world: in fact, 40 nationalities were represented, so it was truly an international school. Every pupil had friends from various countries: whether they came from Burma or Brazil was of little interest to a six-year-old. India was home to all of us, although we were aware that many of our families came from somewhere else. In this kind of atmosphere I never even thought that there was anything unusual about the fact that I was Chinese while my parents were not. My parents had always told me the full story of my adoption, and, although I knew that it was both unusual and real, I just accepted it, I suppose like a child accepts any story.

It was really the move to England which made me fully aware of being a 'Chinese' girl with 'British' parents. I was eight at the time, and we moved into a house near to my grandparents in south Devon. Naturally, being eight years old at the time, I was sent to the local junior school, and I think that it was on my first day at that school that I realised just *how* different I was from everyone else there. I walked to school with a friend whom I had got to know on previous visits to my grandparents, and we waited in the playground for about half an hour before lessons started. I was naturally nervous, starting at a new school, as every child is. However, at previous schools, I had only experienced the curiosity of other pupils because I was *new*. There had been nothing extraordinary about me. I had soon been accepted by the others and had mixed easily with them. But not here. I remember that first morning, in that freezing playground, vividly. Within minutes I was surrounded by what seemed like a vast group of children, all pushing at each other to get a good view of me. My friend pulled me back up some steps behind us because we were being pushed around. It seemed as if I was on a stage, on show for all to see. Questions were hurled at my friend: 'Where's she come from?' 'Does she speak English?' 'How d'you know her then?' My friend, obviously embarrassed by all the attention we had attracted, wasn't able to say anything. The interest in me was not intended to hurt: it was sheer curiosity on the part of children who, living in a small south Devon village, had probably never seen a non-Caucasian before. The hurtful comments came more or less at secondary-school level.

We moved to Hertfordshire and I started at our local comprehensive school. Being much closer to London and therefore to a more racially mixed community, the schoolchildren there were obviously more practised in prejudice, and were well-versed in the terms of racial abuse. The hurtful comments that were directed at me at the comprehensive have been a large problem that both my sister and I have had to come to terms with. However, in schools, little boys will always find something to tease you about, whether you have big ears, red hair or an unusual name. So, although I'm convinced that much of what my sister and I suffered from (my sister still does in fact) was real prejudice, a proportion of the teasing we suffered was only from bored and immature young boys who had nothing more interesting to do.

I am now in the sixth form of different school (a girls' school) and, as soon as I moved, I noticed a different attitude amongst those pupils around me. I have, in the past year, encountered little prejudice, none of it in school. The only slight hazard is that of walking down the main street of our town, where I'm likely to encounter someone (often a teenage boy) who will mutter some racist remark under his breath as he passes me. My sister and I have learned over the years not to react in the slightest when faced with a group of youngsters all shouting abuse at us. An angry reaction will only provoke them to more taunting, and, faced with no reaction they are most likely to get bored and stop. At least, that's what we hope.

Adoption: the inside story

The fact that I was not born to my parents has never, ever, worried or saddened me: with loving and caring parents as I am lucky enough to have, whether or not we are related by blood does not matter to any of us. I feel that my sister and I belong as much to our parents as any of my friends do to their 'natural' parents. My reaction, when asked what I feel about my other family in another country, is that I don't have another family: I've only ever known one mother, one father and one sister. We are all able to talk very freely about my sister's and my first families but they seem so distant, hardly connected with us at all. It seems slightly unreal to me. Maybe I *should* feel closer to my first parents. I don't know. After all, it was thanks to them that I am part of a very close family now. I hope they don't miss me; I hope they are able to speak about me as I am able to speak about them. Although I was born to them and I knew them for nine months, I feel it's not so much who you're born to, it's who you spend your life with that matters.

1982 (*Rebecca, aged 17*)

Naomi, Jean, Rebecca and Marc.

Further reading

A considerable number of books have been published on adoption and related topics. More extensive book lists are obtainable from PPIAS, but the following are particularly recommended:

Hedi Argent, *Find Me a Family* (London, Souvenir Press, 1984)

Cecilia M Brebner, John D Sharp and Frederick H Stone, *The Role of Infertility in Adoption* (London, British Agencies for Adoption and Fostering, 1985)

John Fitzgerald, *Understanding Disruption* (London, British Agencies for Adoption and Fostering, 1983)

John Fitzgerald, Bill and Brenda Mercer, *Building New Families Through Adoption and Fostering* (Oxford, Basil Blackwell, 1982)

Peter and Diane Houghton, *Unfocused Grief: Responses to Childlessness* (Birmingham, National Association for the Childless, 1977)

Claudia Jewett, *Adopting the Older Child* (USA, Harvard Common Press, 1978)

Claudia Jewett, *Helping Children Cope with Separation and Loss* (London, Batsford/BAAF, 1984)

Jill Krementz, *How It Feels to be Adopted* (London, Gollancz, 1984)

Catherine Macaskill, *Against the Odds: Adopting a Mentally Handicapped Child* (London, BAAF, 1985)

Jane Rowe, *Yours by Choice* (London, Routledge & Kegan Paul, 1982)

Barbara Tizard, *Adoption: A Second Chance* (London, Open Books, 1977)

Useful addresses

British Agencies for Adoption and Fostering
11 Southwark Street, London SE1 1RQ
(01-407 8800)

Down's Syndrome Association
12—13 Clapham Common Southside
London SW4 7AA
(01-720 0008)

Family Rights Group
6-9 Manor Gardens, Holloway Road,
London N7 6LA (01-272 4231/2)

Harmony (a group to promote racial harmony and to combat racism)
22 St Mary's Road, Meare,
Near Glastonbury, Somerset (Meare Heath 311)

National Association for the Childless
318 Summer Lane, Birmingham (021-359 4887)

National Association of Young People in Care
2nd floor, The Wool Exchange, Market Street,
Bradford BD1 1LD (0274 728484)

National Foster Care Association
Francis House, Francis Street, London SW1
(01-828 6266/7)

National Organization for the Counselling of Adoptees and their Parents
3 New High Street, Headington,
Oxford OX3 5SJ
(0865 750554, Mon, Wed, Fri, 10—4)

One Parent Families
255 Kentish Town Road, London NW5
(01-267 1361)

Parent to Parent Information on Adoption Services
Lower Boddington, Daventry,
Northamptonshire NN11 6YB
(0327 60295)

Voice of the Child in Care
60 Carysfort Road, London N8
(01-267 1361)

Index

adopted children:
  on being adopted, 164-74
  on tracing natural parents, 90-7
adoption panel, 1, 6
adoption parties, 157-8
affection, inability to accept or show, 29, 35, 36, 42, 60, 61, 64, 65, 66
aggression (in teenager), 36-7
alienation, feelings of, 23-4
Anders, Rebecca, *A Look at Prejudice and Understanding*, 105
anxiety symptoms (in toddlers), 30, 31-2
arguments in the home: effect on institutionalized children, 113-114
assessment interviews, 1, 2-4, 7, 22
attention-seeking, 50, 64, 125-8

bedwetting, 37, 41, 48, 76, 131
Be My Parent (book), 6, 7
black children, adopting: *see* transracial adoptions
blind child, adopting a, 135-6
bonding, 25, 61-70
  and adoptive father, 23
books about adoption, 74
Brazilian baby, adopting a, 8-10
breakdown of adoption: *see* disruption
breastfeed, desire to, 25
Brodzinsky, David: 'New perspectives on adoption revelation', 71
brothers and sisters:
  adopting as group, 52-6
  attitudes to newly adopted child, 45-51
  keeping in touch with, 78, 84-5
  twins, 57-60

cheating at games, 50
child guidance clinics, 43
Children's Act 1975 (section 26), x, 89, 90
colour prejudice, adult, 102, 103
commitment to new family, lack of, 36, 38
contested adoptions, 138-45
  appeals, 140-1
  costs of hearing, 140, 142
  dispensing with mother's consent, 142
  handing back a child, 144-5
  length of process, 143, 144

deaf children, coping with, 12, 15-17, 130-2
decision-making: inability of institutionalized children, 42-3, 114
depression (in teenager), 37
discipline, importance of, 35, 36, 50, 66
disruption, 146
  due to behavioural problems, 147-9, 155
  due to effect on other children, 147, 148, 149-50, 155
  teenager 151-4
Dr Barnardo's, adopting from, 6-7
Donley, Kay, 146
Down's Syndrome babies, adopting, 12-13, 25-7, 137, 161-2

eating problems 37, 48, 117
eldest, adopting a child as the, 48, 49, 51, 148-9
enuresis: *see* bedwetting

Index

fathers, adoptive, 25-7, 51
  child's difficulties in forming relationship with, 49, 62, 64, 114
  immediate bond with adopted child, 23, 24
  as single parent, 136-7

Gill, Owen and Jackson, Barbara, *Adoption and Race*, 98, 99
grandparents, keeping in touch with, 81, 83
guardian ad litem, 8, 130
guardianship, 130
guilt:
  at disrupted adoptions, 146, 148, 150, 153
  at initial inability to love child, 23-4, 64, 65

handicapped children, adopting, 11, 12, 19-20
  agency for: *see* Parents for Children
  blind, 135-6
  deaf, 12, 15-17, 130-2
  Down's Syndrome, 12-13, 25-7, 137, 161-2
  mentally handicapped, 5, 11, 12, 83-4
  spastic, 17-19
  spina bifida, 13-15
health visitor, support from, 22-3
hearing aids, 16-17
home studies, 8-10
hypochondria, 30, 32-3, 48-9

immaturity in teenagers, 38, 43, 117
inadequacy, feelings of, 22, 23
insecurity, symptoms of, 30, 31-2, 41, 46, 147, 167-8
institutionalized children, 111-118
  effect of arguments on, 113-14
  inability to make decisions, 42-3, 114
  inability to make relationships, 116
  inability to play, 115
  limited vocabulary, 112, 115, 123
  lying, 117-18
  material possessions, disregard for, 41-2, 116, 117
  possessiveness with toys, 112, 167
  and present-giving, 113
  self-orientation, 114
  stealing, 117, 158
  tidiness, 112, 113
  see also teenagers, adopting
interviews, assessment, 1, 2-4, 7, 22

Jackson, Barbara: *see* Gill, Owen

local authority:
  adoption units, 11
  allowances, 43-4
  services, 5-6, 43
love, initial inability to, 23-4, 33, 64, 65
lying (of institutionalized children), 117-18

memories, importance of early, 73-4
  compiling life-story book, 75, 78, 79-80
mentally-handicapped children, adopting, 5, 11, 12, 83-4
  see also Down's Syndrome babies
mixed-race children, adopting: *see* transracial adoptions
mongols: *see* Down's Syndrome babies
mothers, natural: *see* natural family

name, new:
  reluctance of child to use, 63
  reluctance of school to use, 124
National Deaf Children's Society, 16

Index

natural family:
  an alcoholic mother, 85-6
  contested adoptions, 138-45
  keeping in touch with, 78, 79-80, 81, 82, 84-5, 143
  meetings with natural mother, 25, 86-8
  retaining contact with grandparents, 81, 83-4
  sharing child with, 82
  telling child about, 42, 63, 71-80
  tracing, 89-97
New Society, 5
nightmares, 30, 67
Nuffield Centre, London, 16

overseas adoption (Brazil), 8-10

'Parents for Children' (agency), 5, 11, 34, 78, 135, 136-7
Parent to Parent Information on Adoption Services: *see* PPIAS
past, importance of the, 71, 75, 78, 79
physical contact, rejection of, 29, 64, 66, 67
play, inability of institutionalized child to, 115
possessions, disregard for, 41-2, 116, 117
possessiveness with toys, 32, 112, 167
Post-Adoption Center for Education (PACER), 89
PPIAS, x, xii
  Newsletter, x, xii
present-giving and institutionalized children, 113

relationships:
  inability to make, 116
  see also affection; bonding
Rowe, Jane, *Yours by Choice*, 71
running away, 158, 159

Sawbridge, Phillida, 34
  on adopting teenagers, 42-4

school, adopted children at, 119-28
  'maladjusted' child, 121-2
  mixed-race children, 100, 120-121, 125, 170
  and new name, 124
  too much understanding, 122-4
  underachievement, 35, 119, 121-2, 168
self-orientation of institutionalized children, 114
sibling groups, adopting, 52-60
single parents, adoption by, 129
  advantages, 130
  disadvantages, 131-2
  unmarried man, 136-7
  unmarried women, 130-6
sleeping problems, 30, 32
Small, John, New Black Families Project, 98
social services department, dissatisfaction with, 5-6
social workers, assessment interviews with, 1, 2-4, 7, 22
spastic child, coping with, 12, 17-19
spina bifida baby, adopting, 13-15
stealing, 35, 117, 158

tantrums, 28, 29, 30, 33, 59, 168
teenagers, adopting, 34-44
  advice on, 42-4
  aggression, 36-7
  bedwetting, 37, 41
  decision-making, 42-3
  depression, 37
  disrupted adoption, 151-4
  eating problems, 37
  expenses, 43-4
  immaturity, 38, 43
  importance of discipline, 35, 36
  inability to accept family commitments, 36, 38
  inability to give or receive affection, 35, 36, 42
  insecurity, 41

Index

    lack of interest and motivation, 35, 41
    sources of support, 43
    stealing, 35
    untrustworthiness, 39
    see also institutionalized children, adopting
telling a child, 71-2
    advice on, 73-4
    books about adoption, 74
    compiling life-story book, 75, 78, 79-80
testamentary guardian, 130
tidiness of institutionalized children, 112, 113
toddlers, adopting, 28-33
    adoptive mother's inability to love, 33
    anxiety symptoms, 30, 31-2
    hypochondria, 30, 32-3
    inability to accept affection, 29
    inability to share, 32
    insecurity, 31-2
    rejection of word 'Mummy', 30
    sleeping problems, 30, 32
    tantrums, 28, 29, 30, 33
tracing natural parents, 72, 89-97
    counselling before, 89
    reasons for child's need, 89, 90, 92, 93
transracial adoptions, 2, 7-8, 46-8, 54-6, 68-70, 98-9
    adult prejudice, 102, 103
    advice on treatment of black child, 104-5
    babies, 23-5
    comments of adopted children, 165, 169-74
    coping with prejudice, 101-2
    emphasis on black culture, 104-5
    feelings of alienation, 23-4
    importance of background, 71, 75
    name-calling, 101, 102
    problems at school, 100, 120-1
    teasing, 101
    toddlers, 29, 30-1, 32-3
twins:
    adopting, 57-60
    meeting as adults, 94-5

underachievement at school, 35, 119, 121-2, 168
unmarried parents: *see* single parents
untrustworthiness, 39

vetting: *see* assessment interviews
vocabulary, limited (of institutionalized children), 112, 115, 123